MY TRUE
Colors

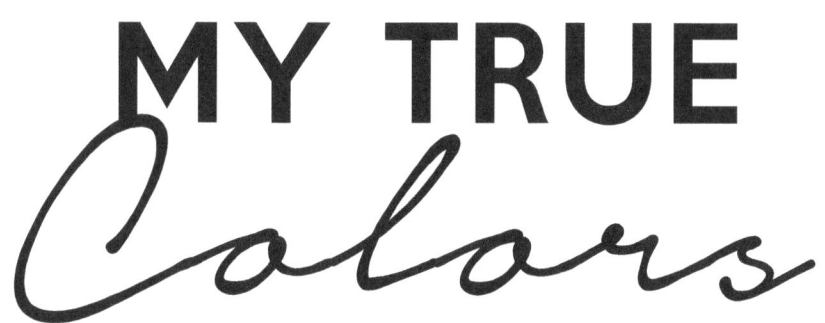

Keep Calm and Color On

Your Own Unique
Coloring Book Retreat

by Caron Chandler Loveless

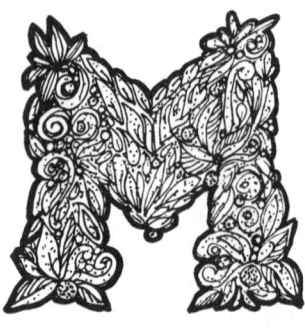# y first memory of art making...

I'm five years old and I'm laying on the floor next to my friend, Stephanie, who lives across the street. We're coloring. She's a few years older and she's showing me how to angle my crayon just-so. *Shading this way will make the colors come out smooth*, she says. *And, outline your picture. It'll make it look better.* I do everything Stephanie says. I like the smell of the crayon, how the waxy color goes on the page, and I like creating with my friend. I'm blissfully happy. And something in my brain decides I should anchor this moment forever.

My next art memory is life-defining. I'm in the sixth grade. Our teacher, Mrs. Higginbotham, has given us an art assignment. We're drawing palm trees. And one by one we come up to her desk to show her our progress. I still remember how I felt standing next to her, hearing her say, "This is really good!"

Trust me. My picture was nothing special. But, her words sparked an eternal flame inside me.

My teachers' simple encouragement made such an impression that I spent every day of my summer vacation that year perfecting the palm tree. In fact, I trace her comment to every artistic endeavor I've attempted since then. And that little sketch sits on a shelf in my hereugostudio office where I see it everyday. It's the only treasure from my childhood I possess and it reminds me: 1) even the smallest words of encouragement can powerfully impact others 2) art makes me happy and 3) not to despise the day of small beginnings.

This book of sketches & quotes you hold is another small beginning for me. It represents the daring venture of gifting my art to you so you can expand it, personalize it and find your own delight in hours of creative expression. Each sketch is hand-drawn, not computer generated. I did have technical help cleaning up the images and I played a little, here and there, with mirroring and multiplying a few sketches but I'm pleased that every page is made by my own hand.

For adding color: I love using felt markers, but my suggestion to you for this book would be to use colored pencils since they're more versatile for shading. Keep a pencil sharpener handy. You'll need a good point to get to the tiny details.

And I'm anxious to see how you finish my drawings! On the back page you'll find my contact information where you can send your pictures, connect with me on social media or get in contact with me.

Thanks so much for choosing this special collection of my art. I had so much fun bringing it to life.

My hope for you is many hours of carefree bliss as you make each piece your very own. I love that, much like with my friend all those years ago, you and I will now be co-creators, joined together in magical, mystical moments of making art.

Grace & peace always~

Caron Chandler Loveless
hereugostudio.com

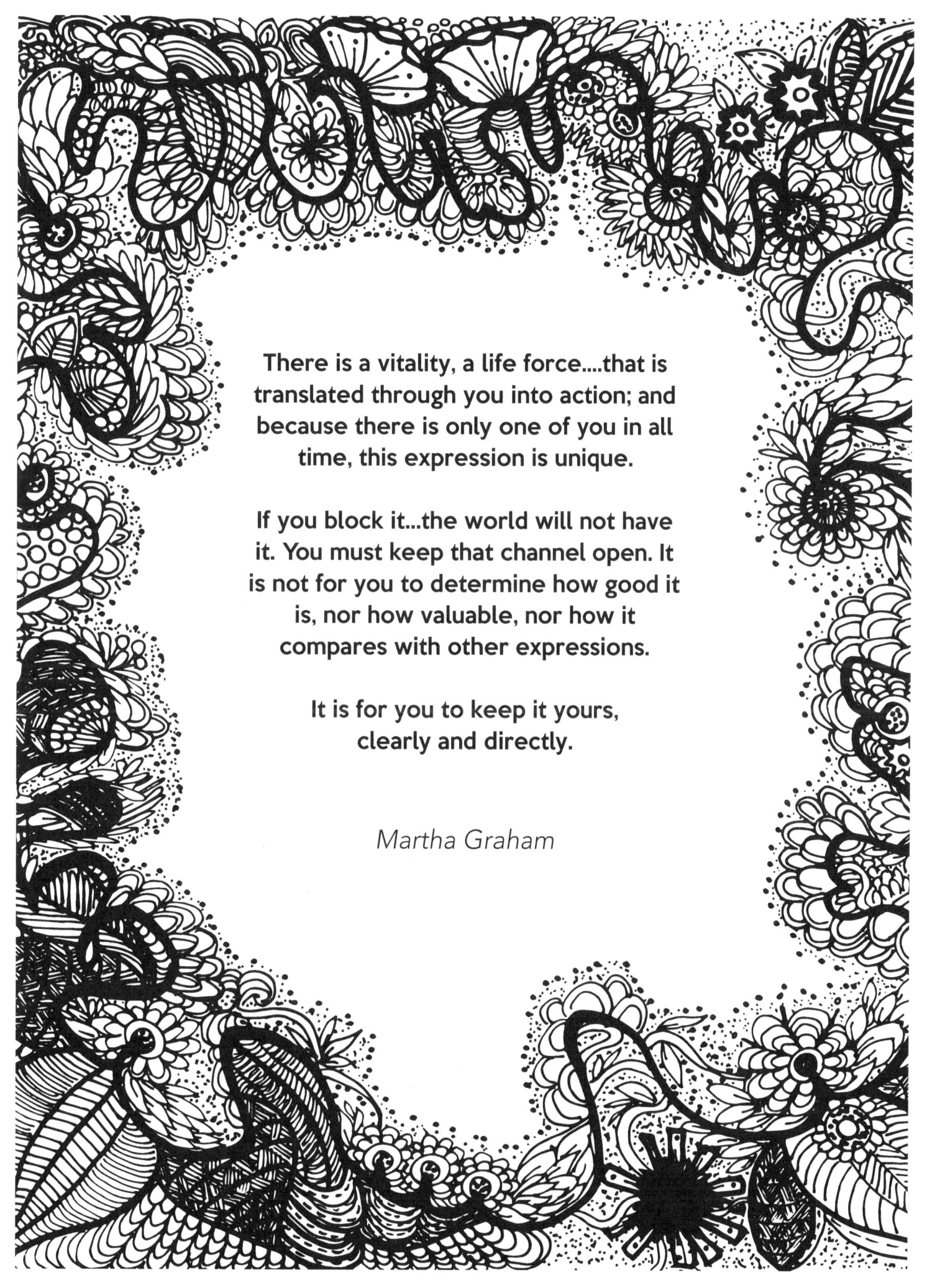

There is a vitality, a life force....that is translated through you into action; and because there is only one of you in all time, this expression is unique.

If you block it...the world will not have it. You must keep that channel open. It is not for you to determine how good it is, nor how valuable, nor how it compares with other expressions.

It is for you to keep it yours, clearly and directly.

Martha Graham

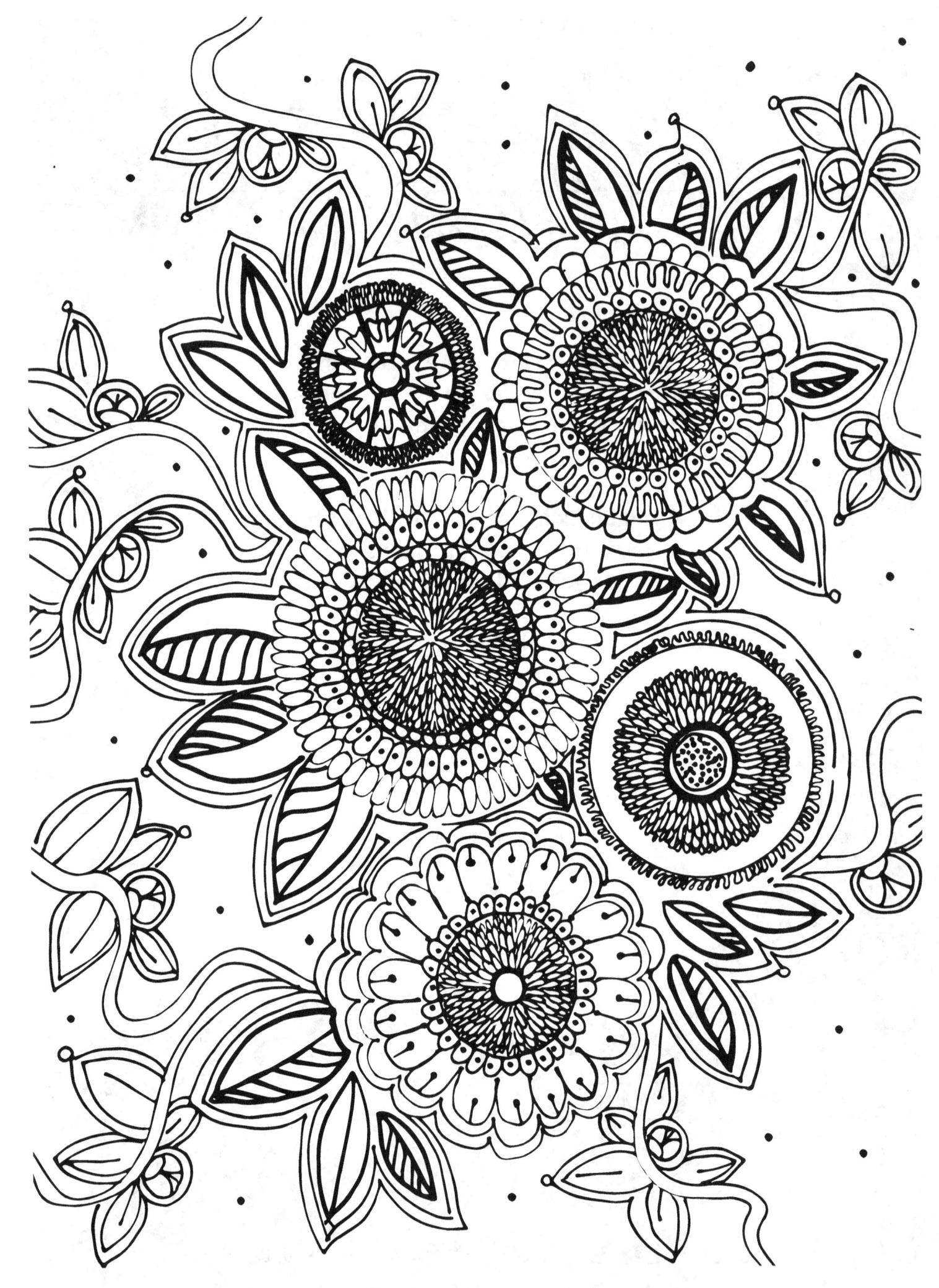

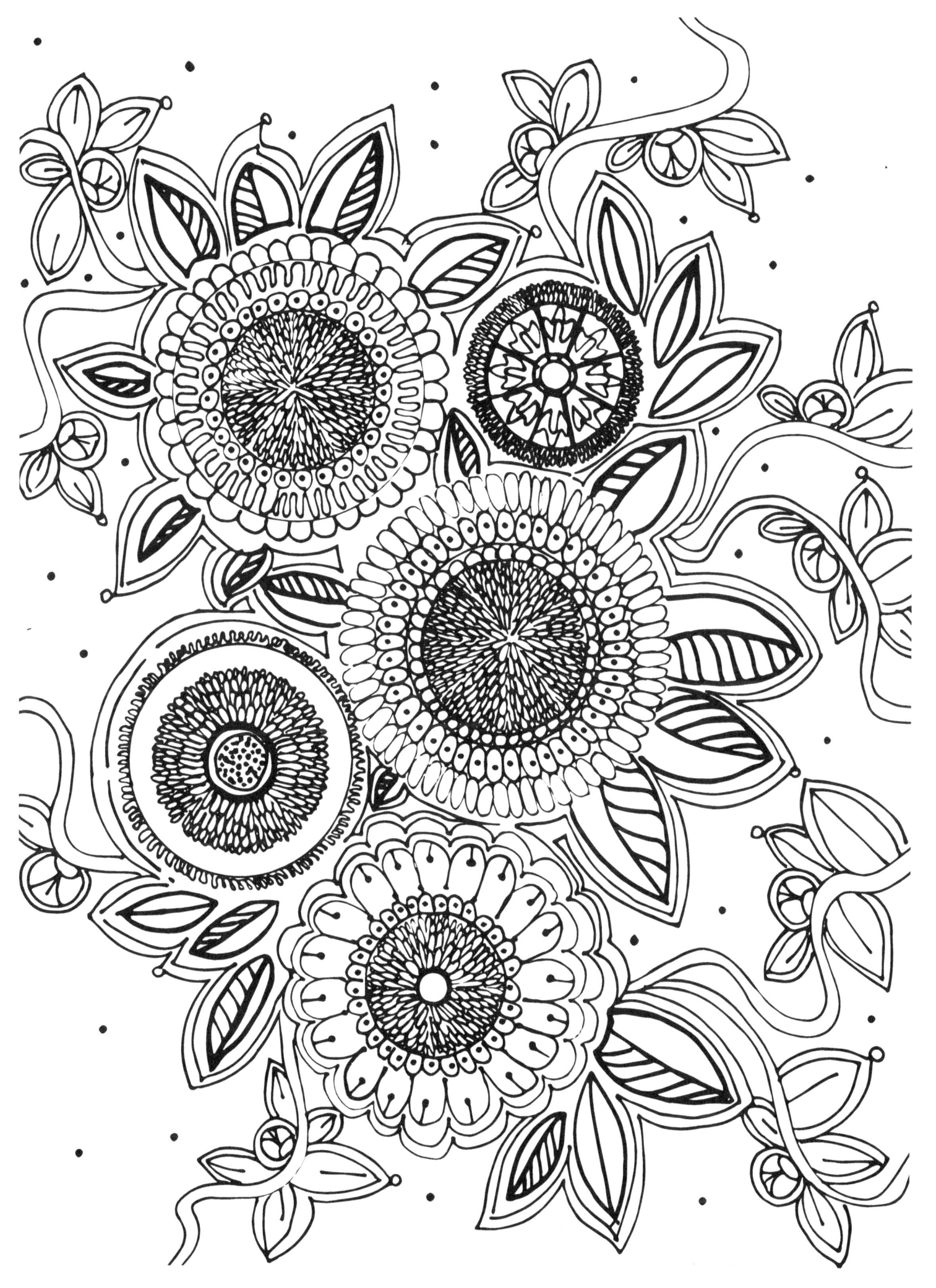

Good art is not what it looks like but what it does to us.

Roy Adzak

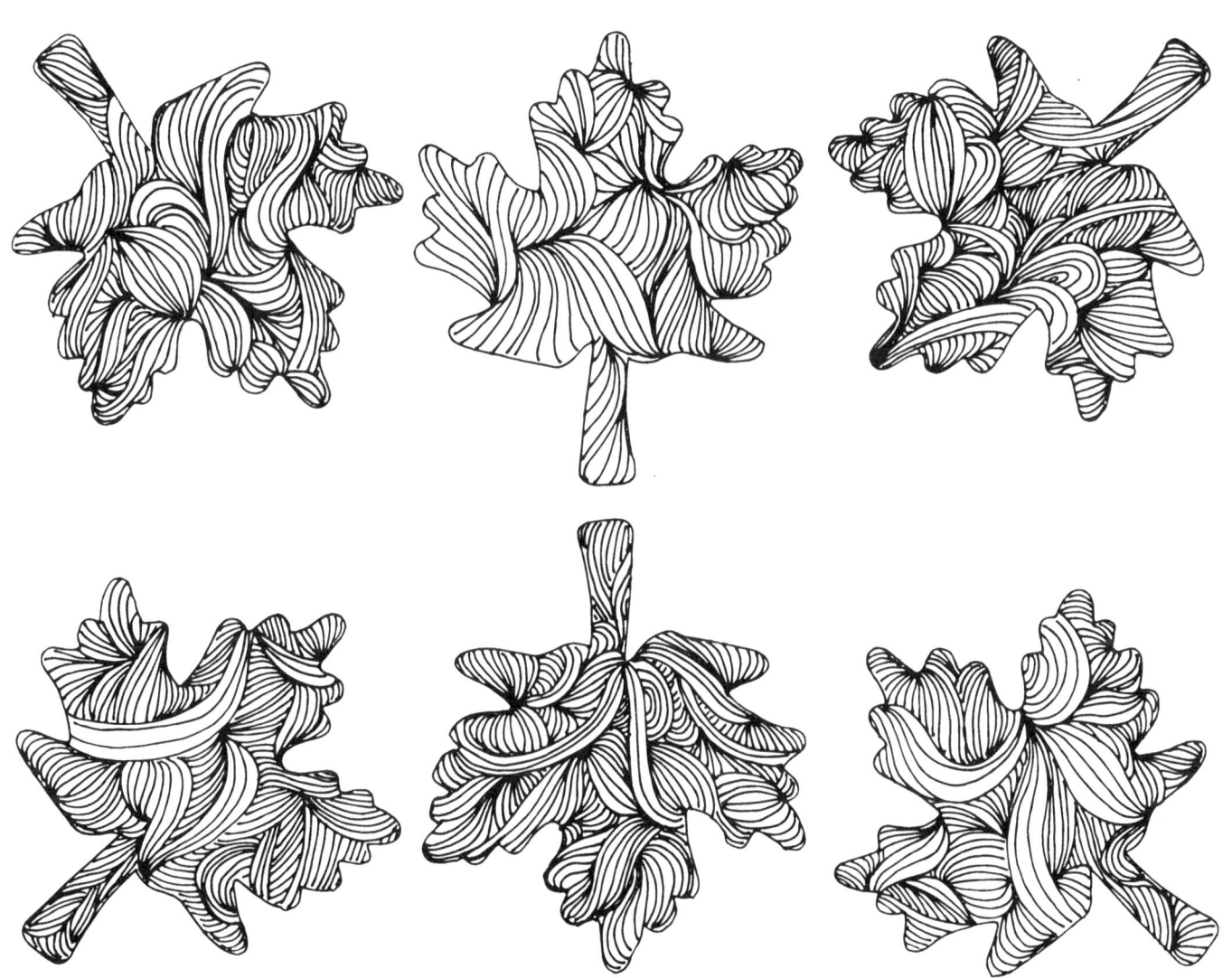

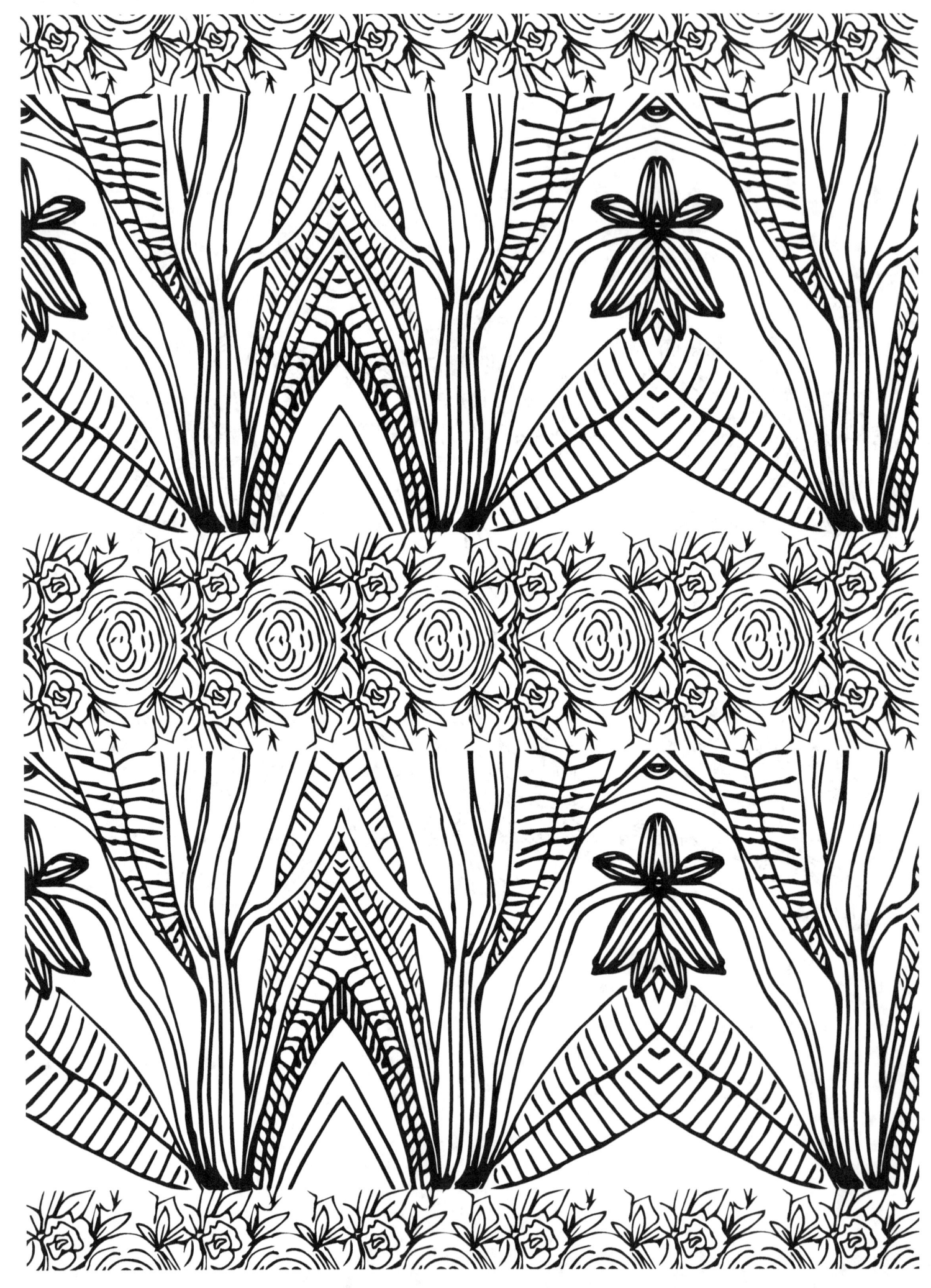

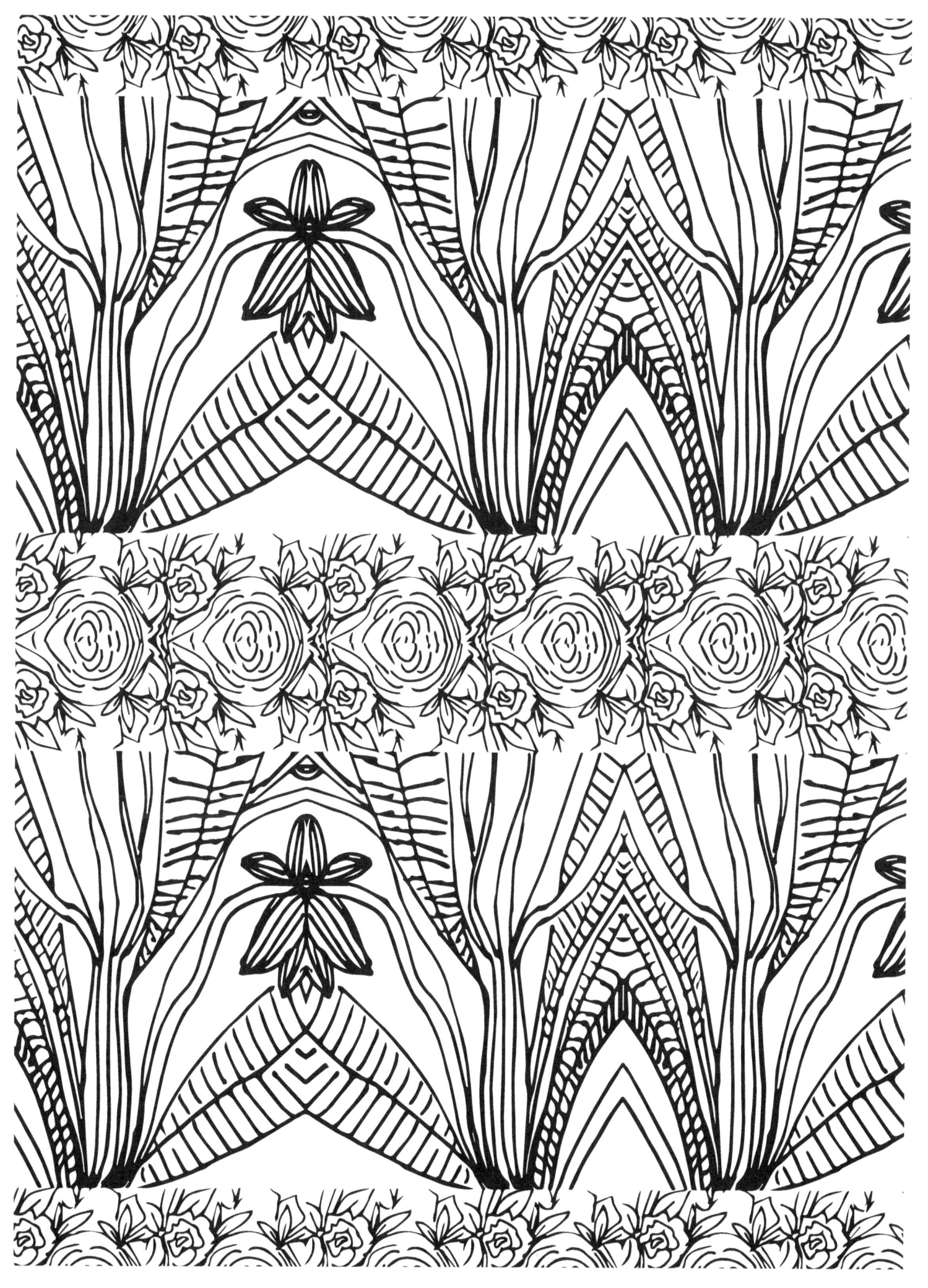

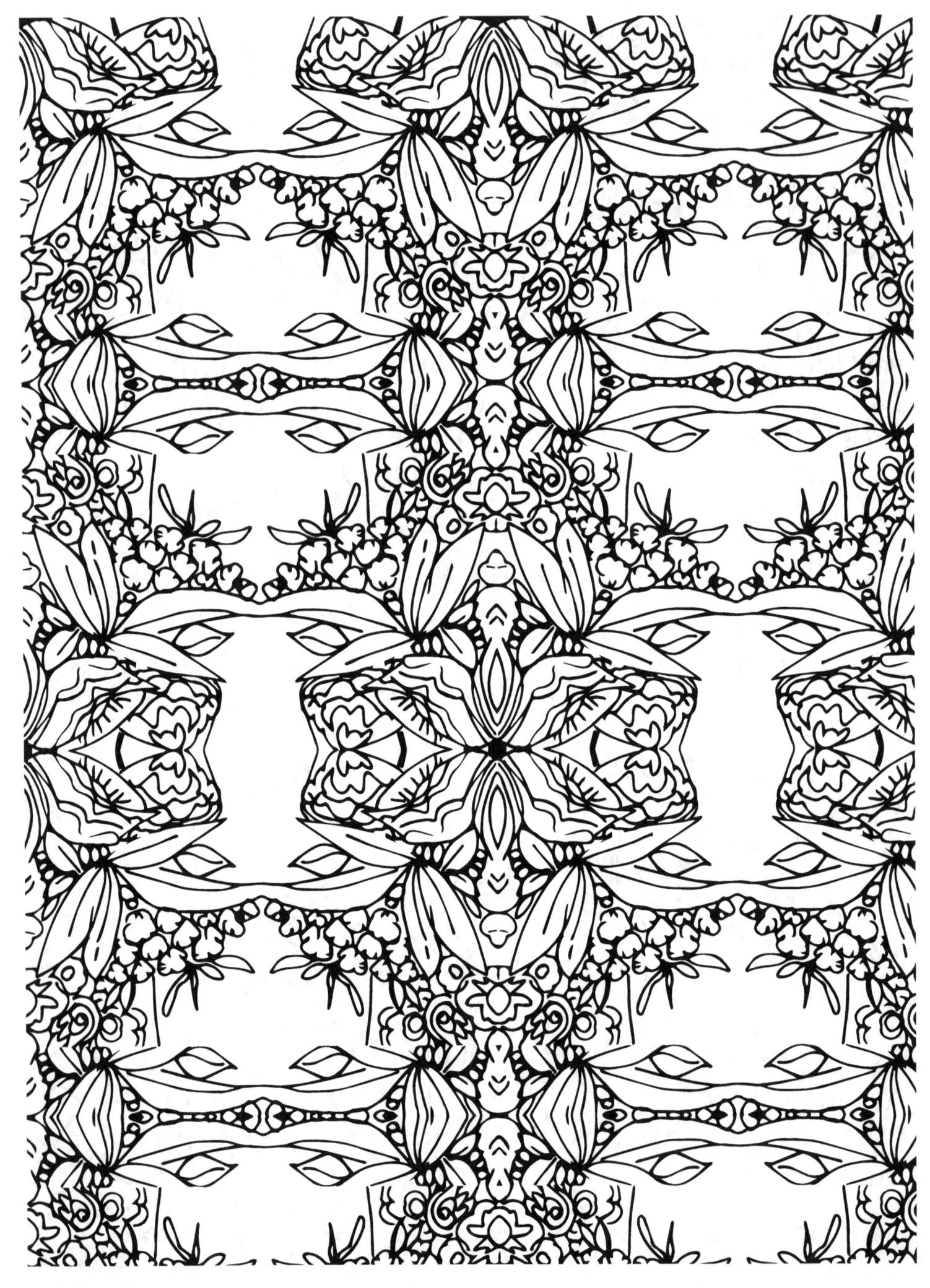

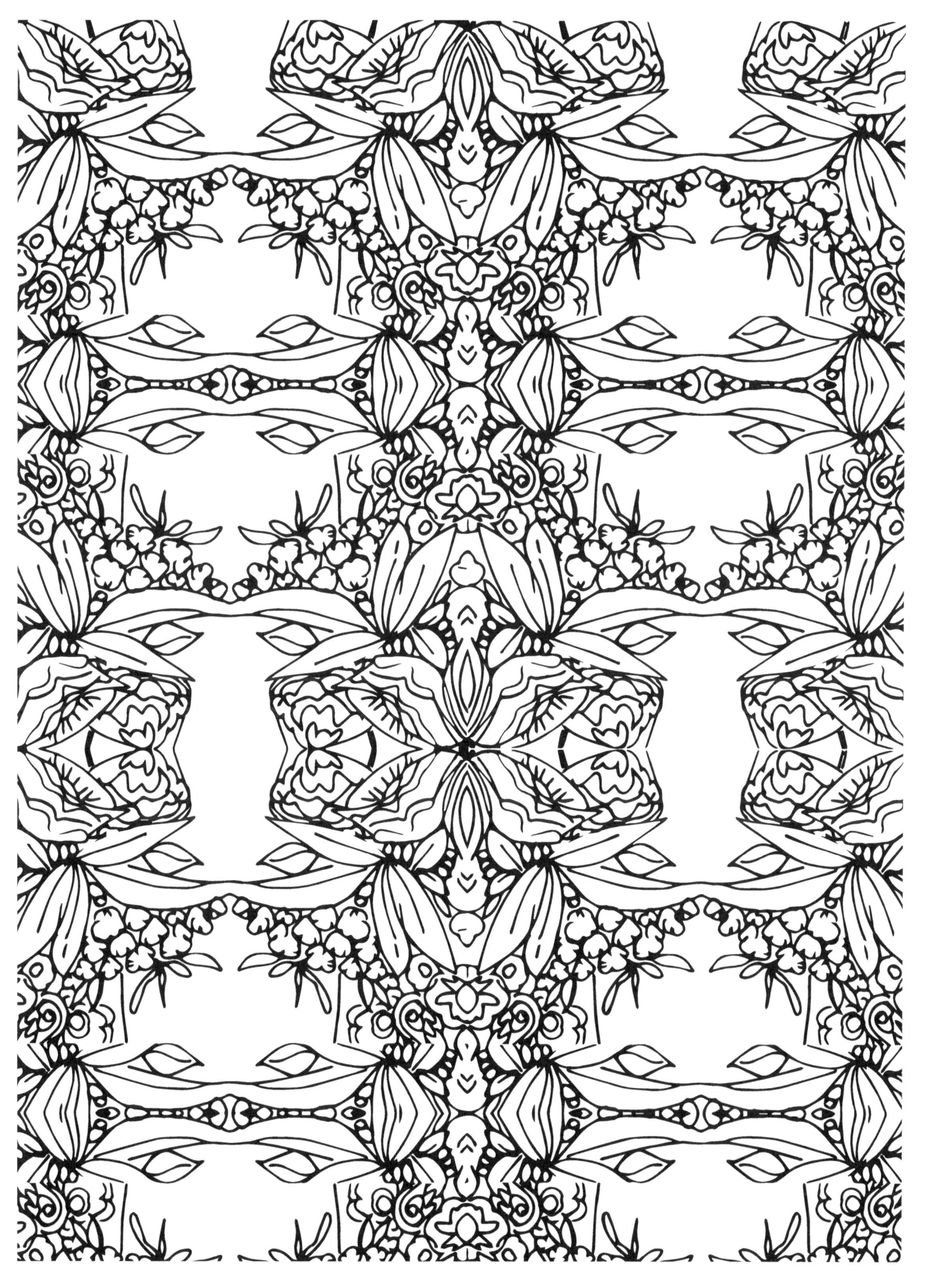

**If art doesn't make us better then
what on earth is it for?**

Alice Walker

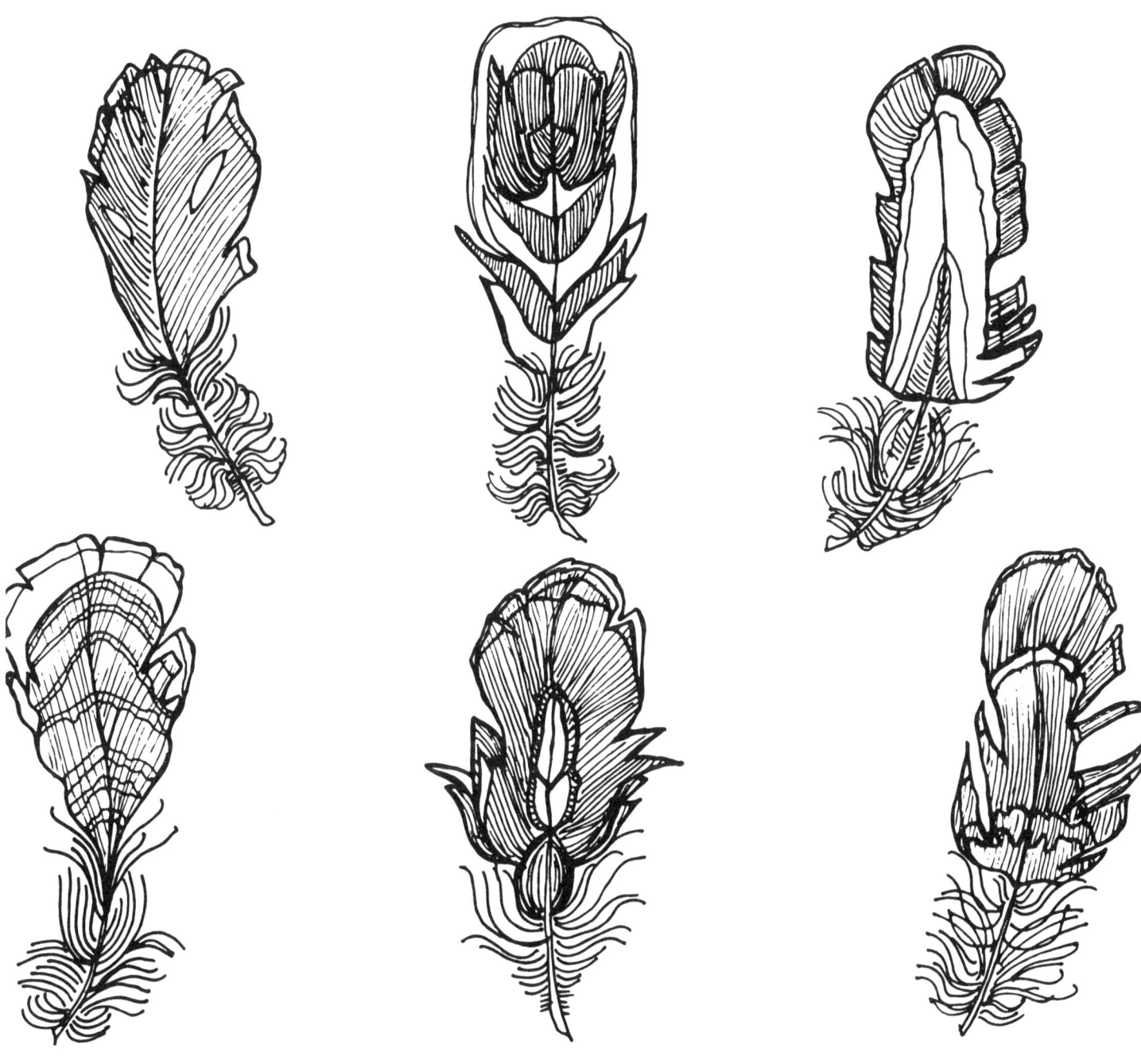

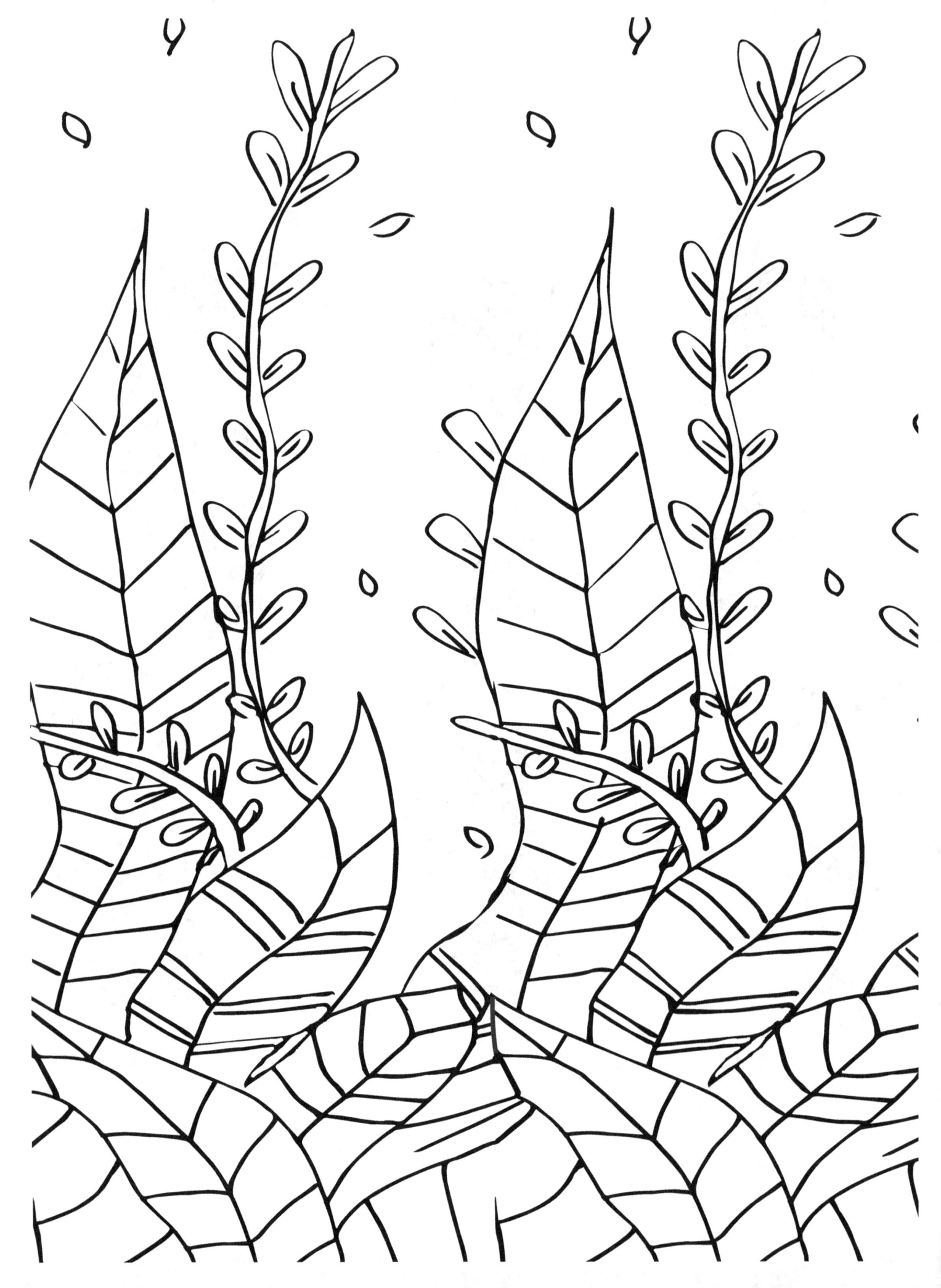

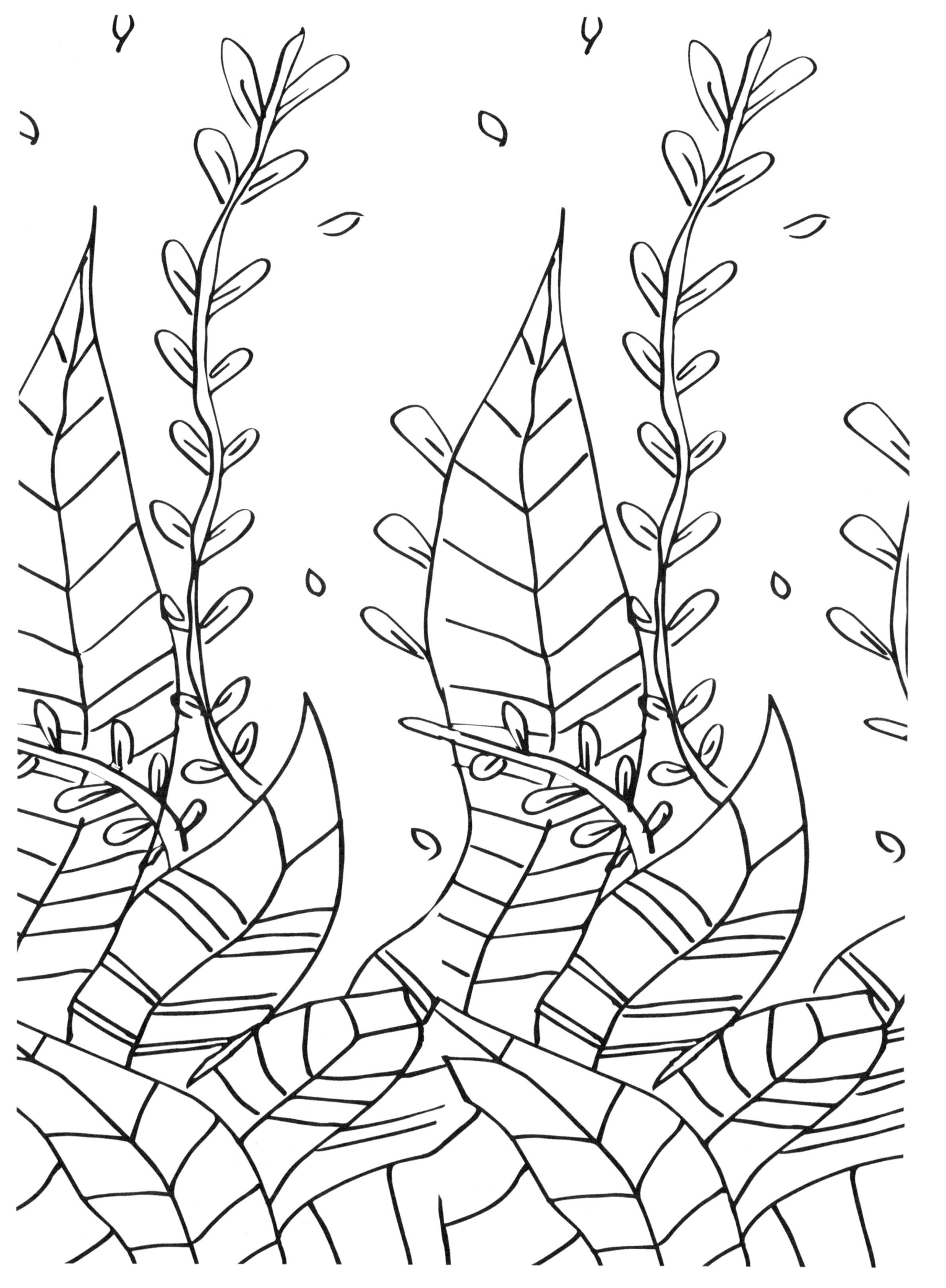

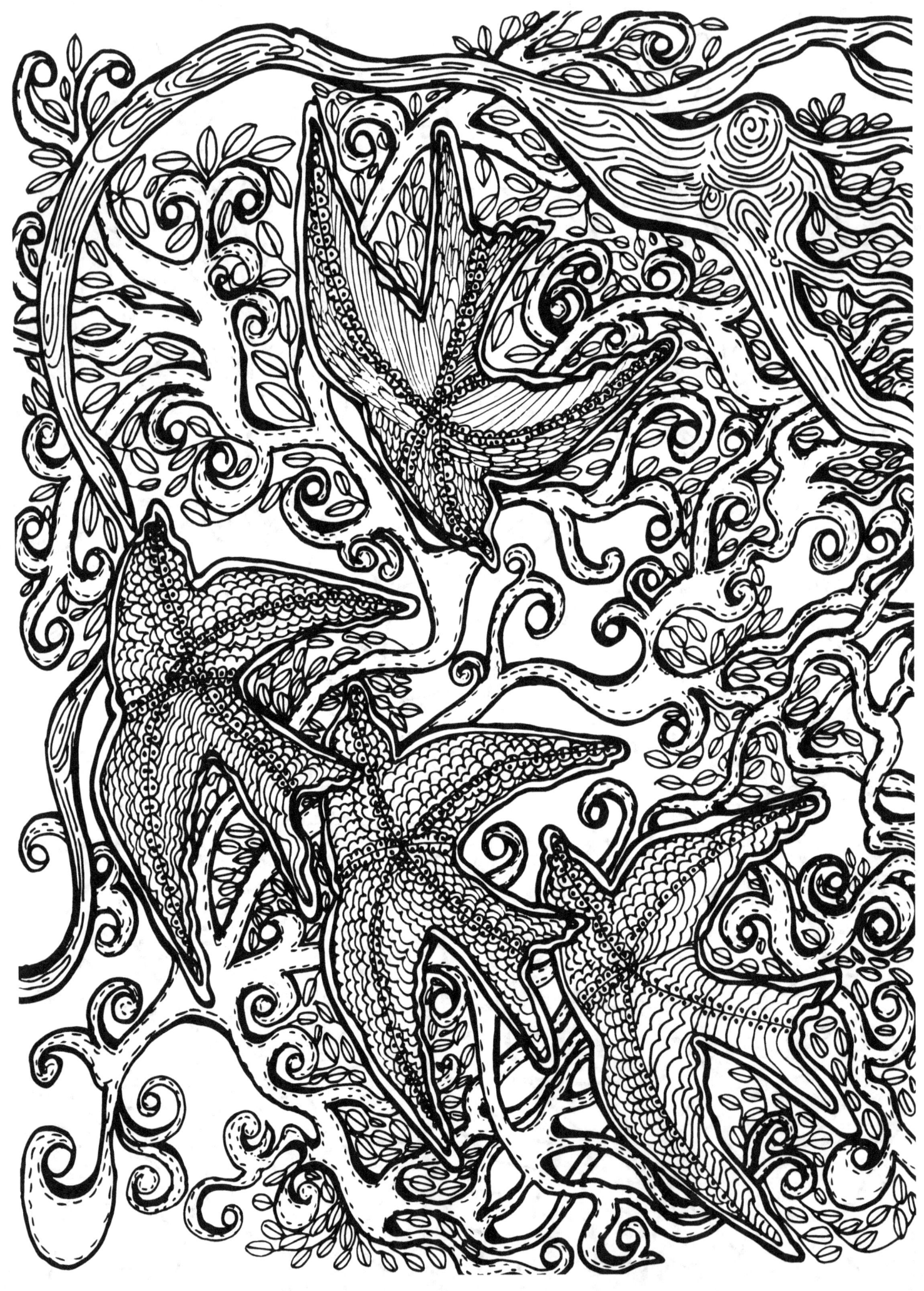

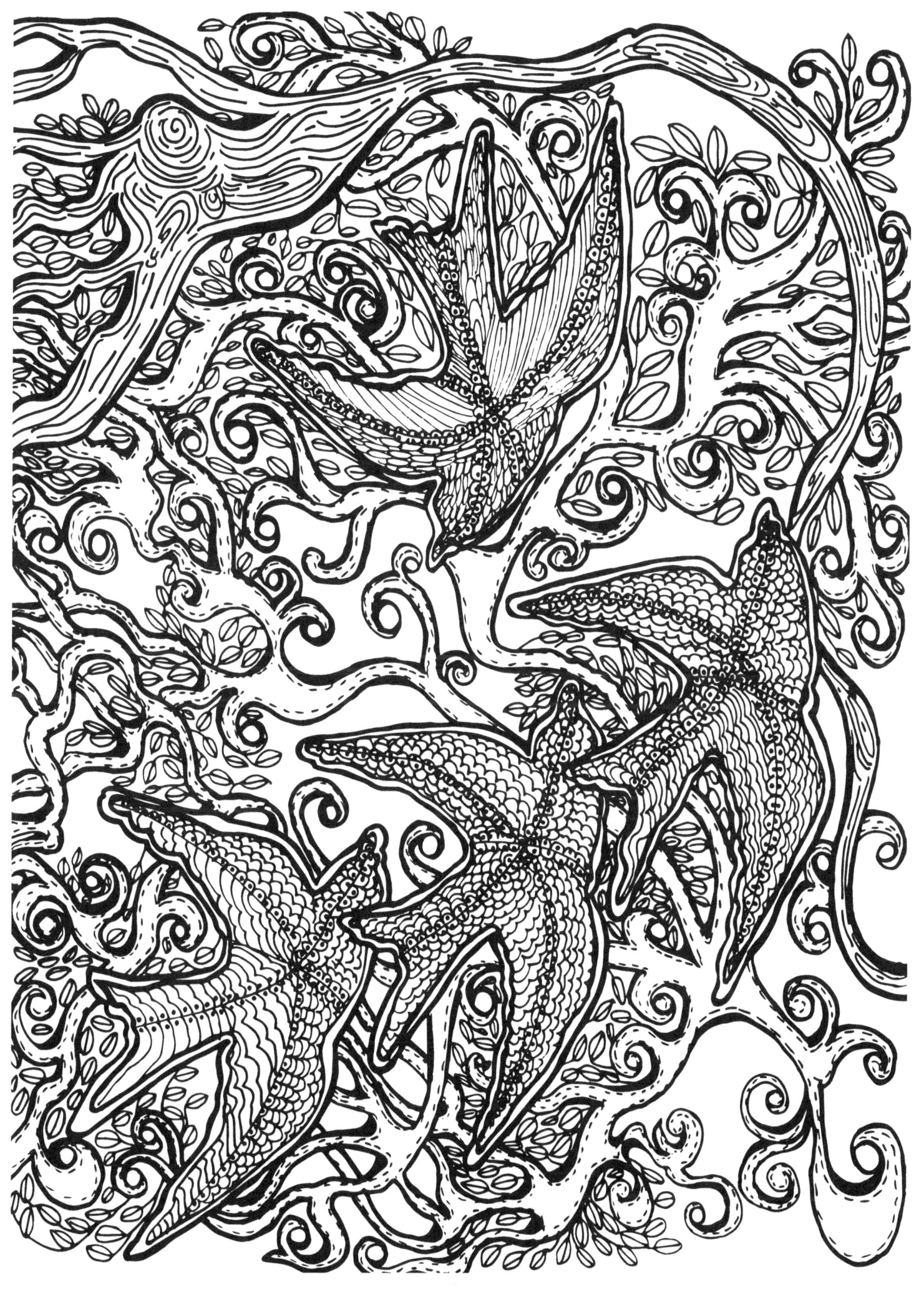

**Art washes away from the soul
the dust of everyday life.**

Picasso

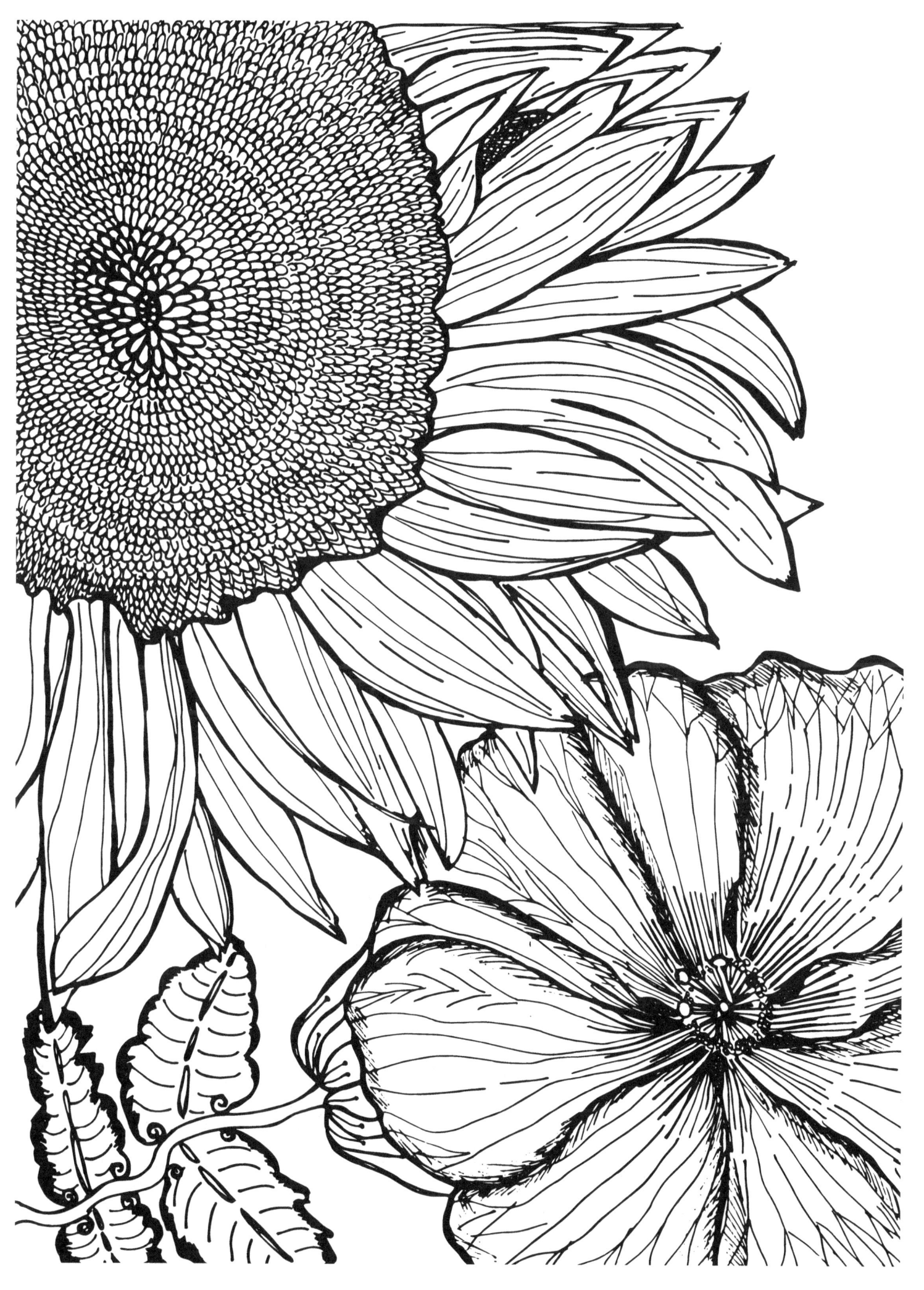

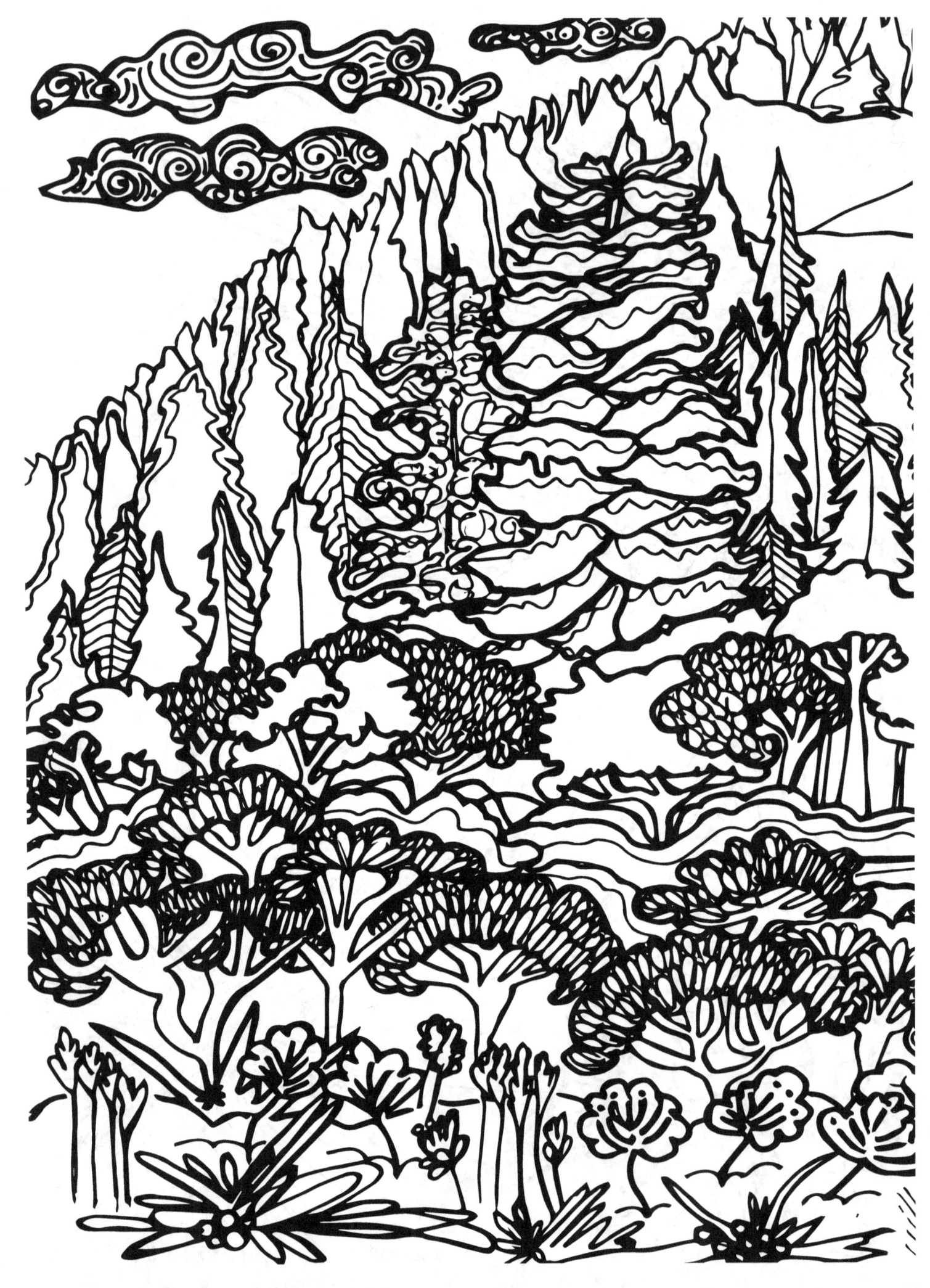

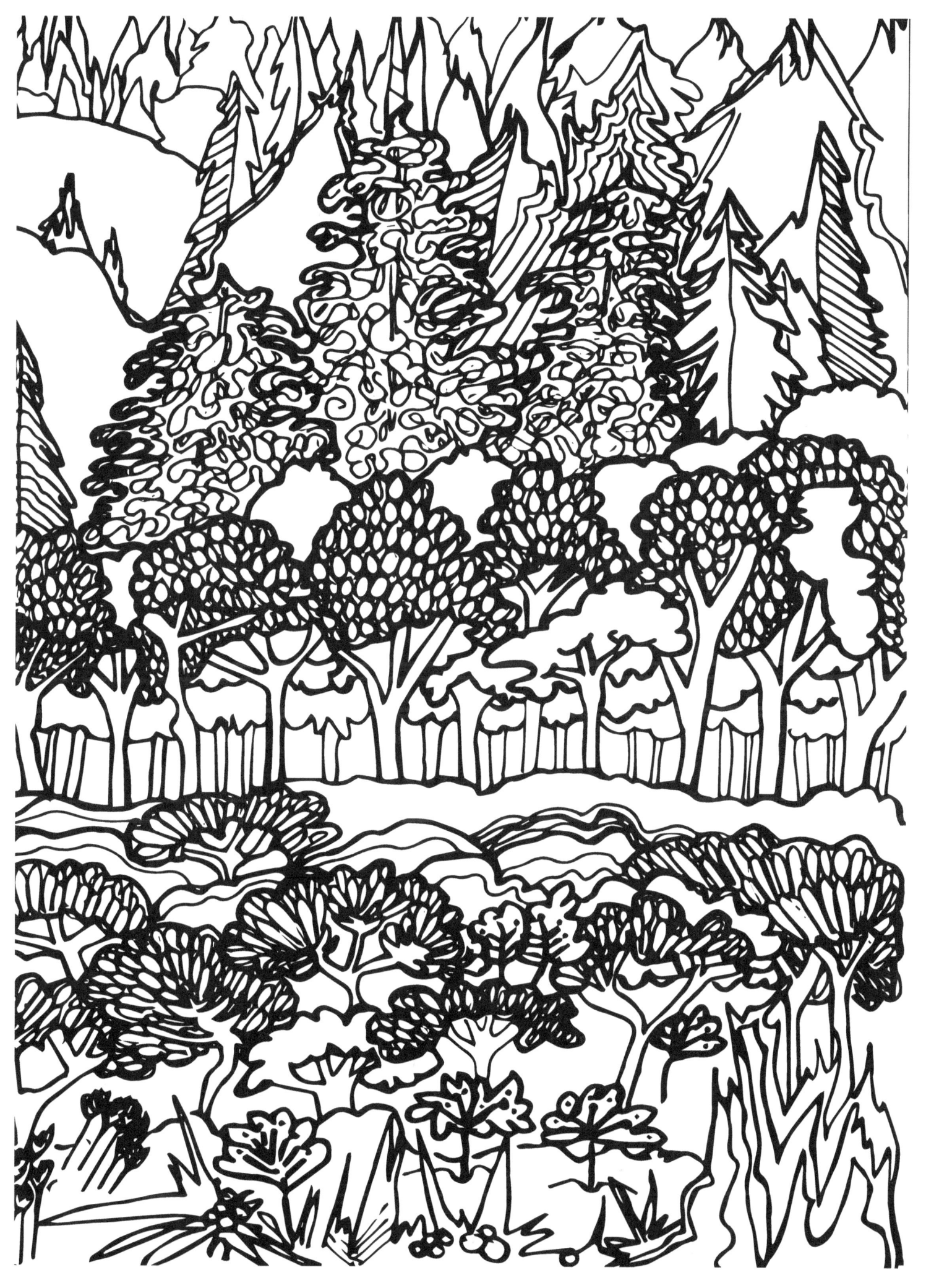

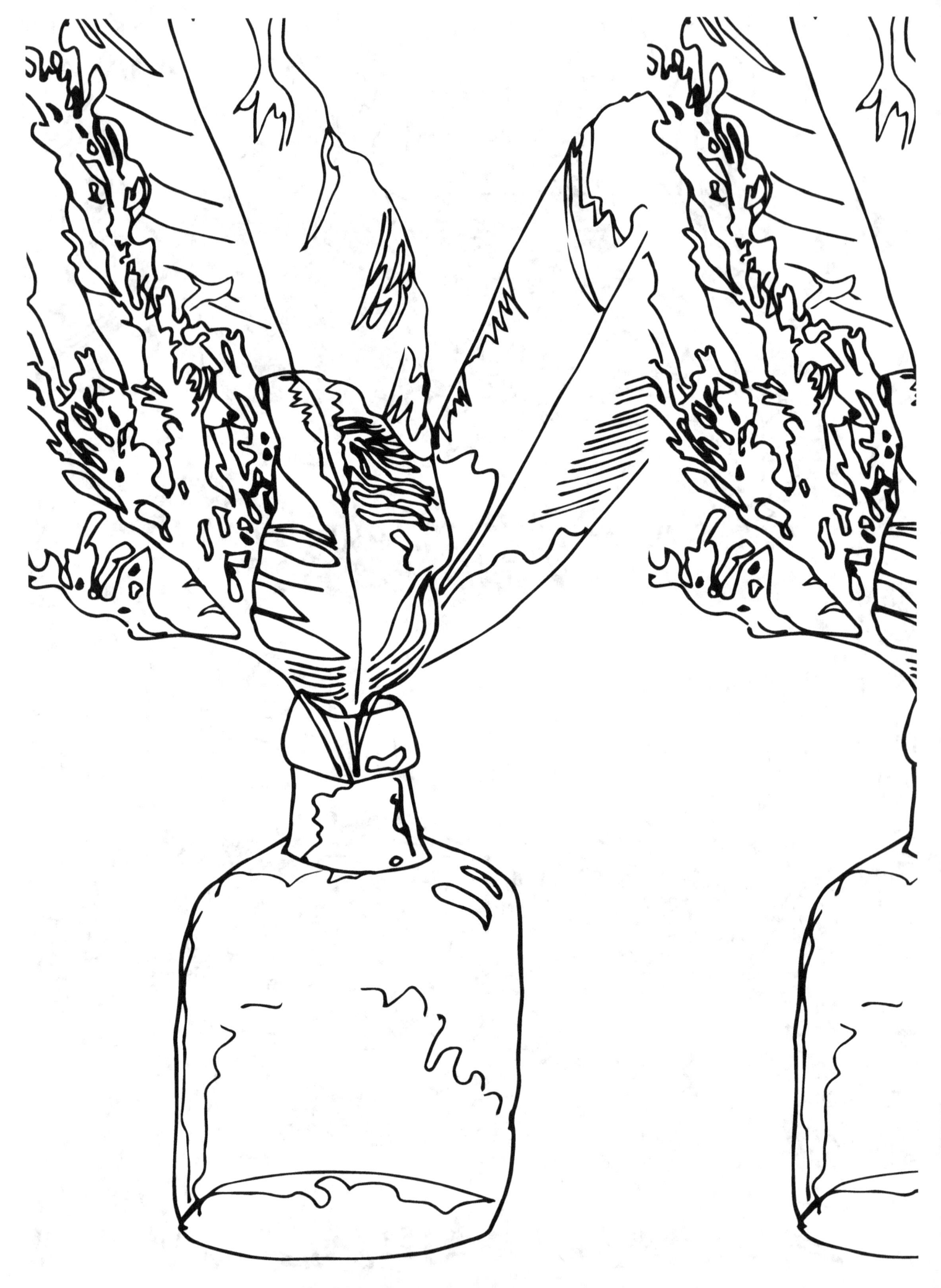

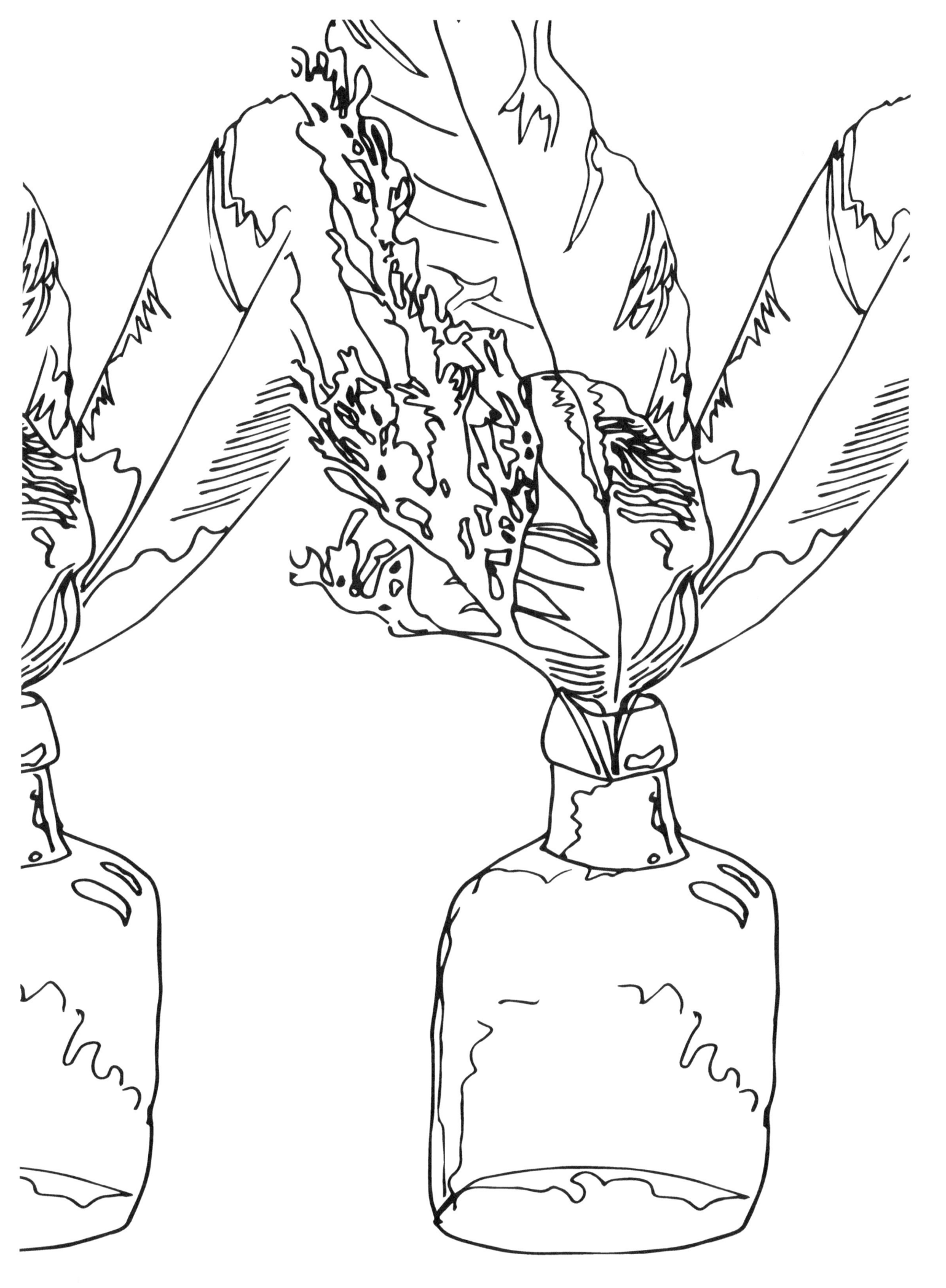

Life beats down and crushes the soul and art reminds you that you have one.

Stella Adler

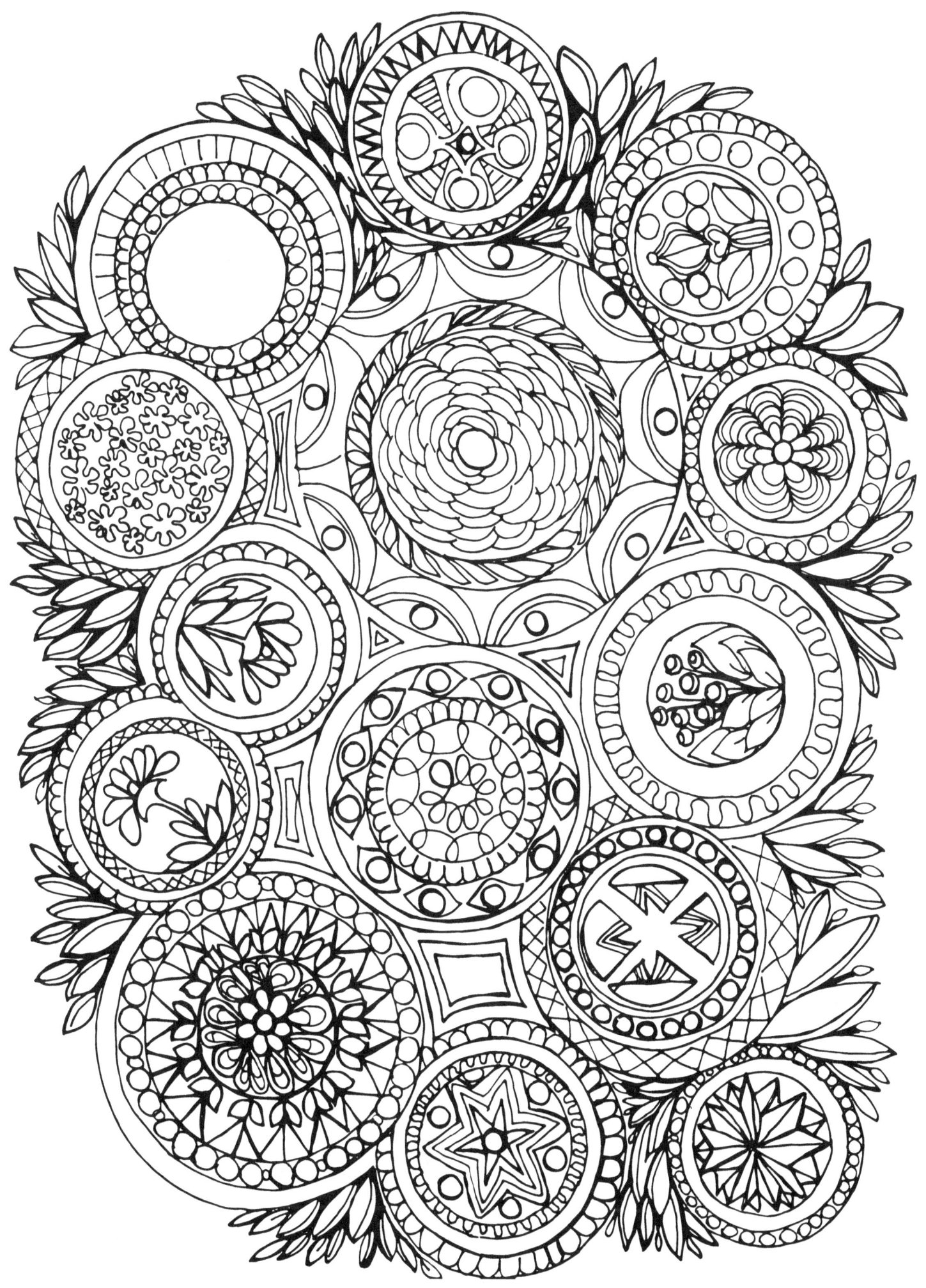

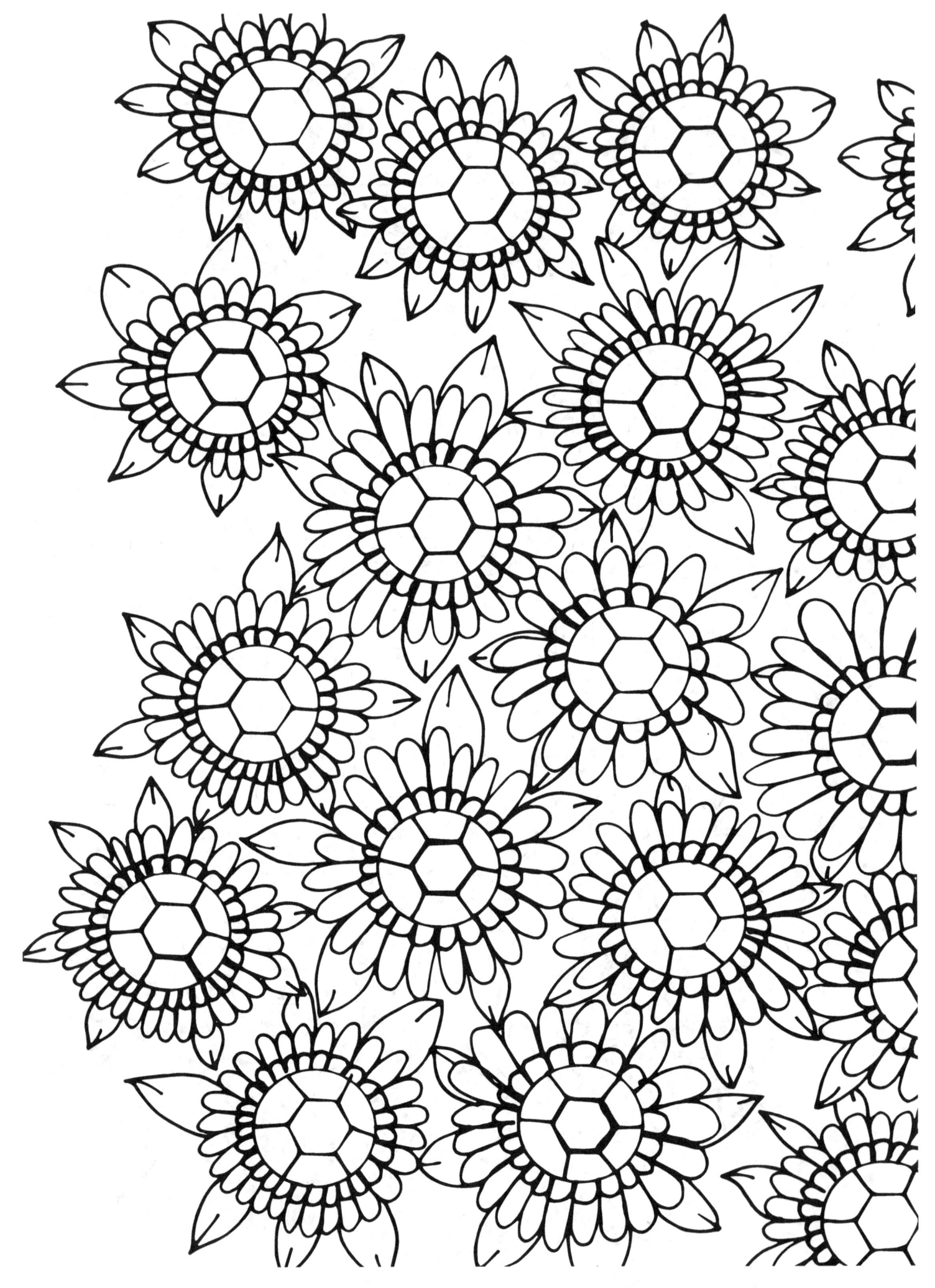

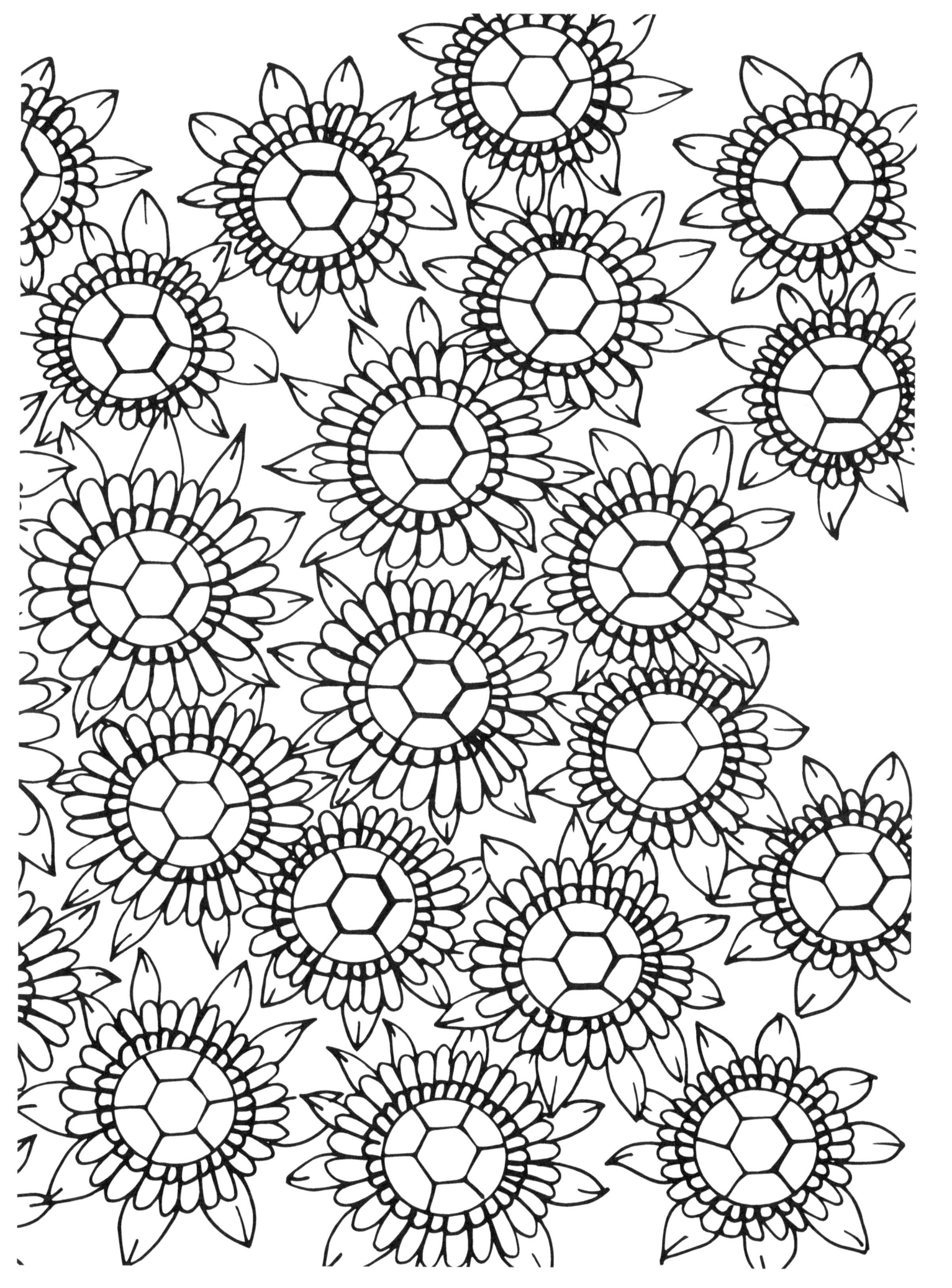

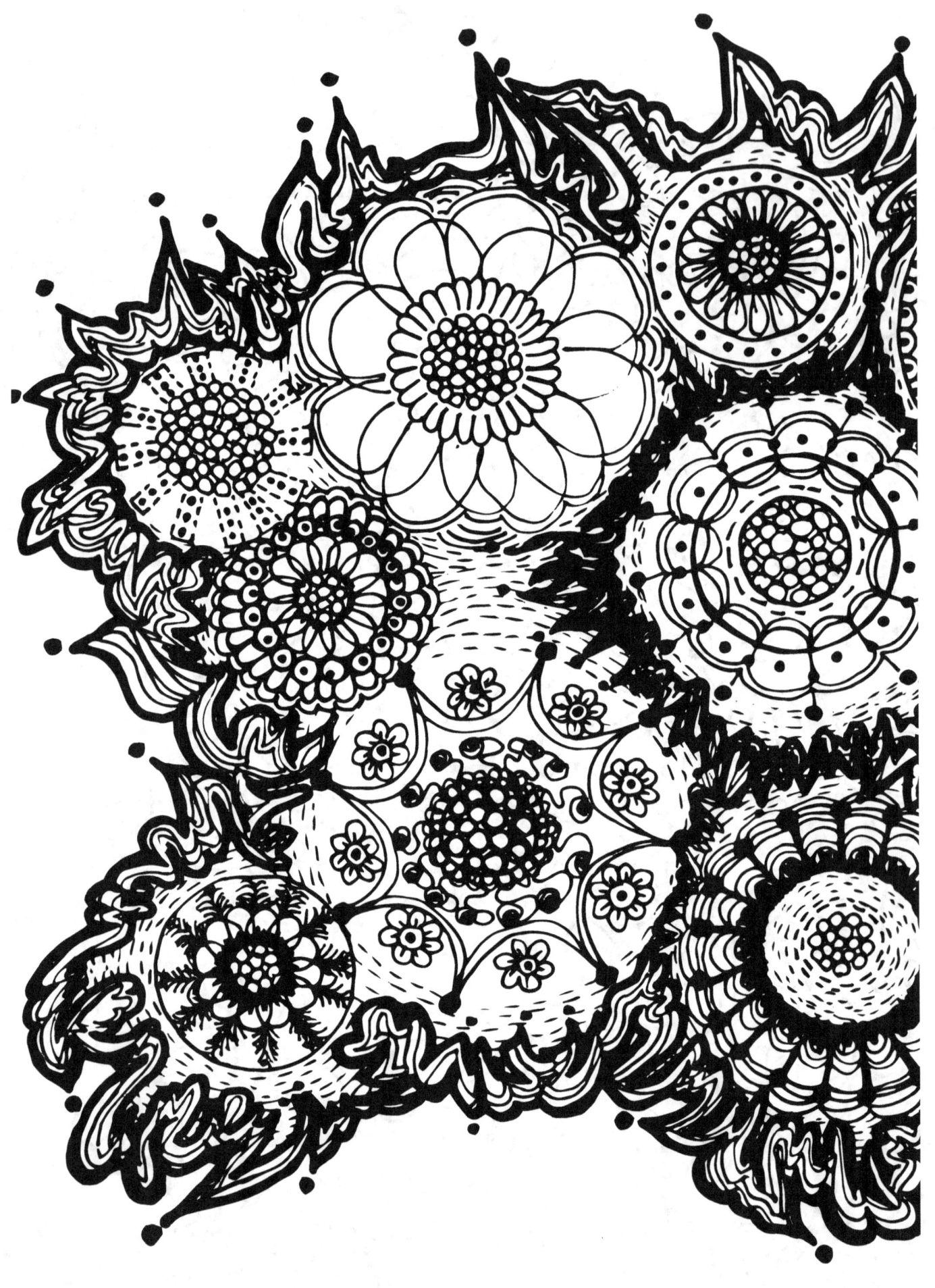

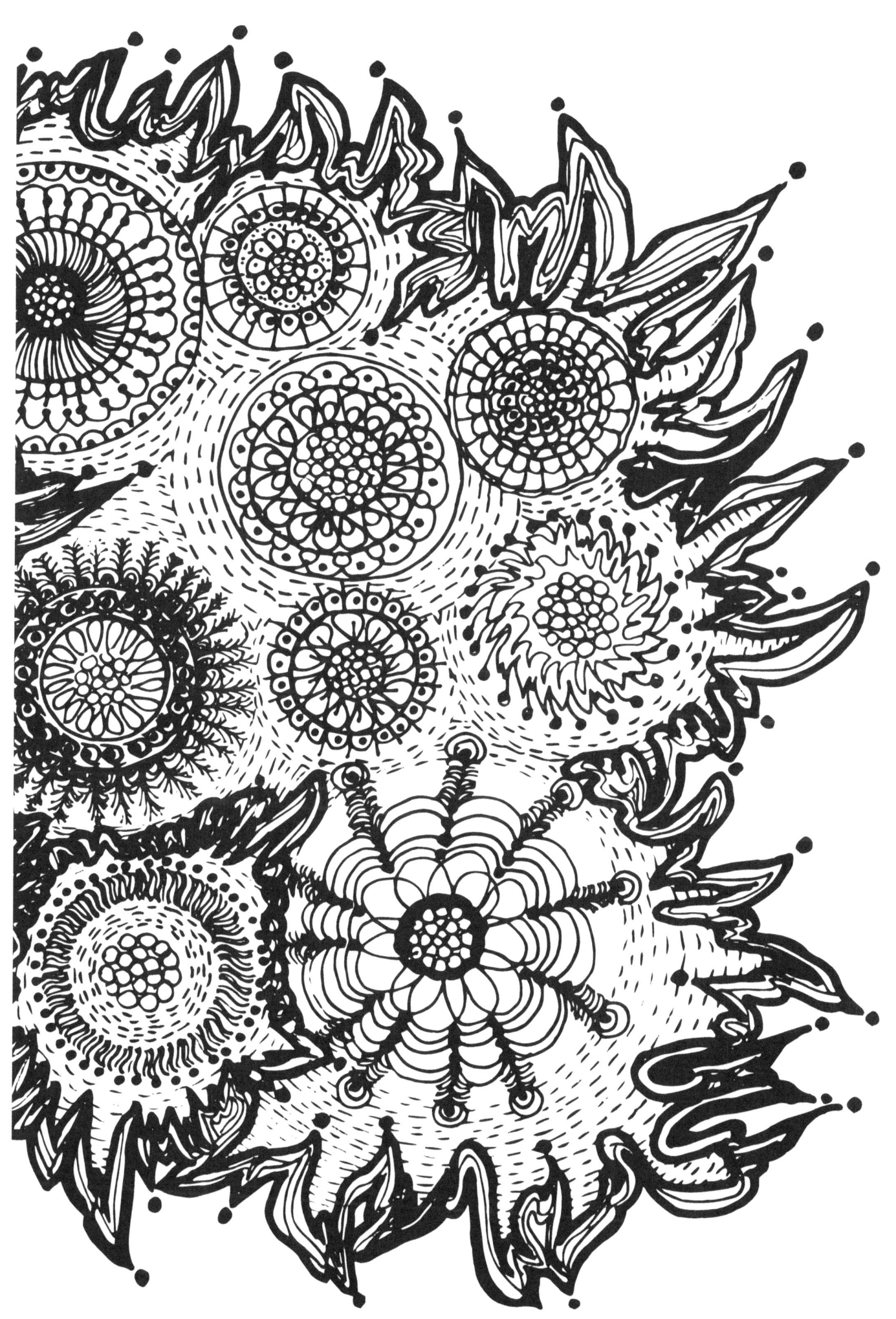

There can be no set rule laid down for the making of pictures.

Robert Henri

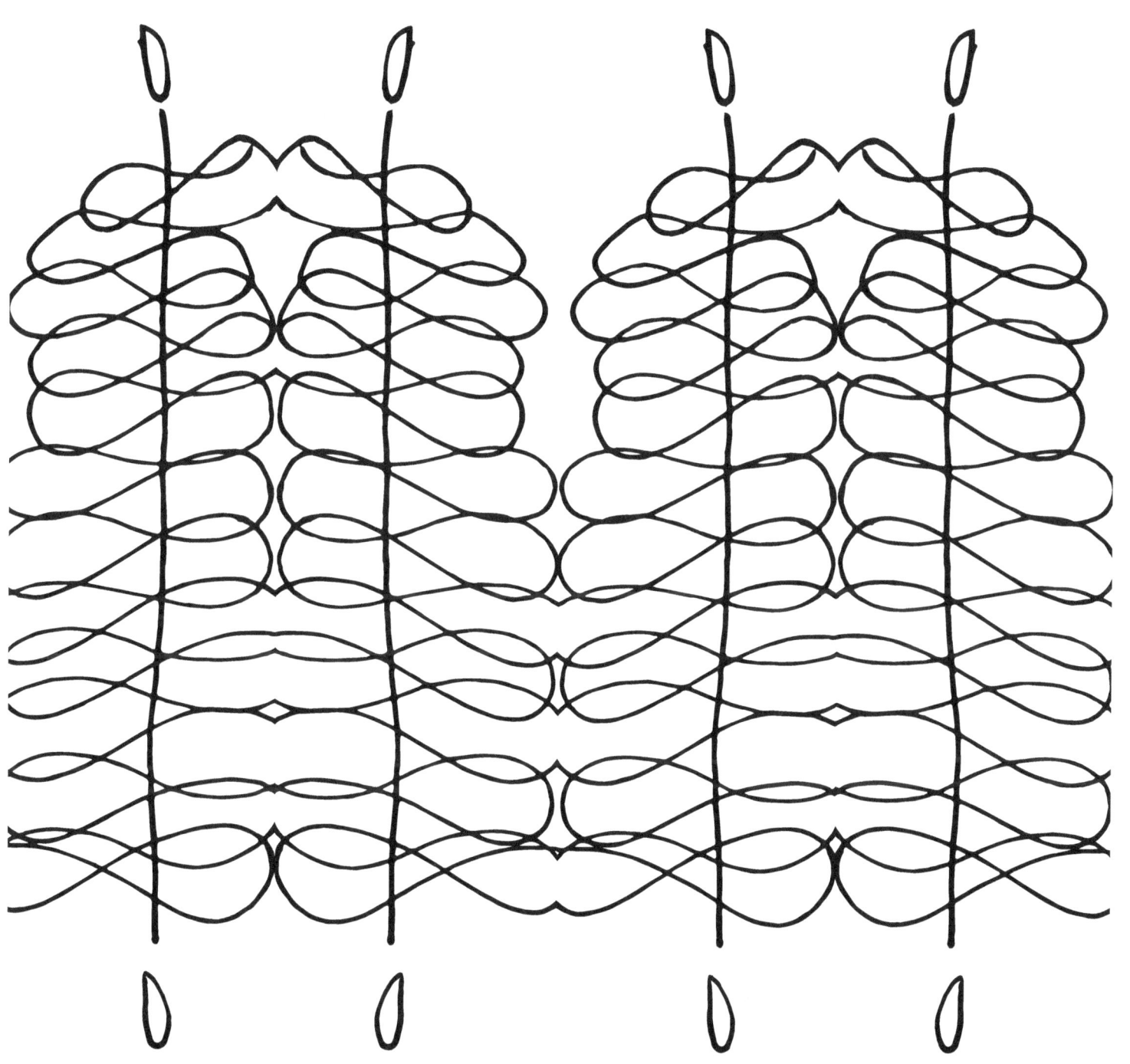

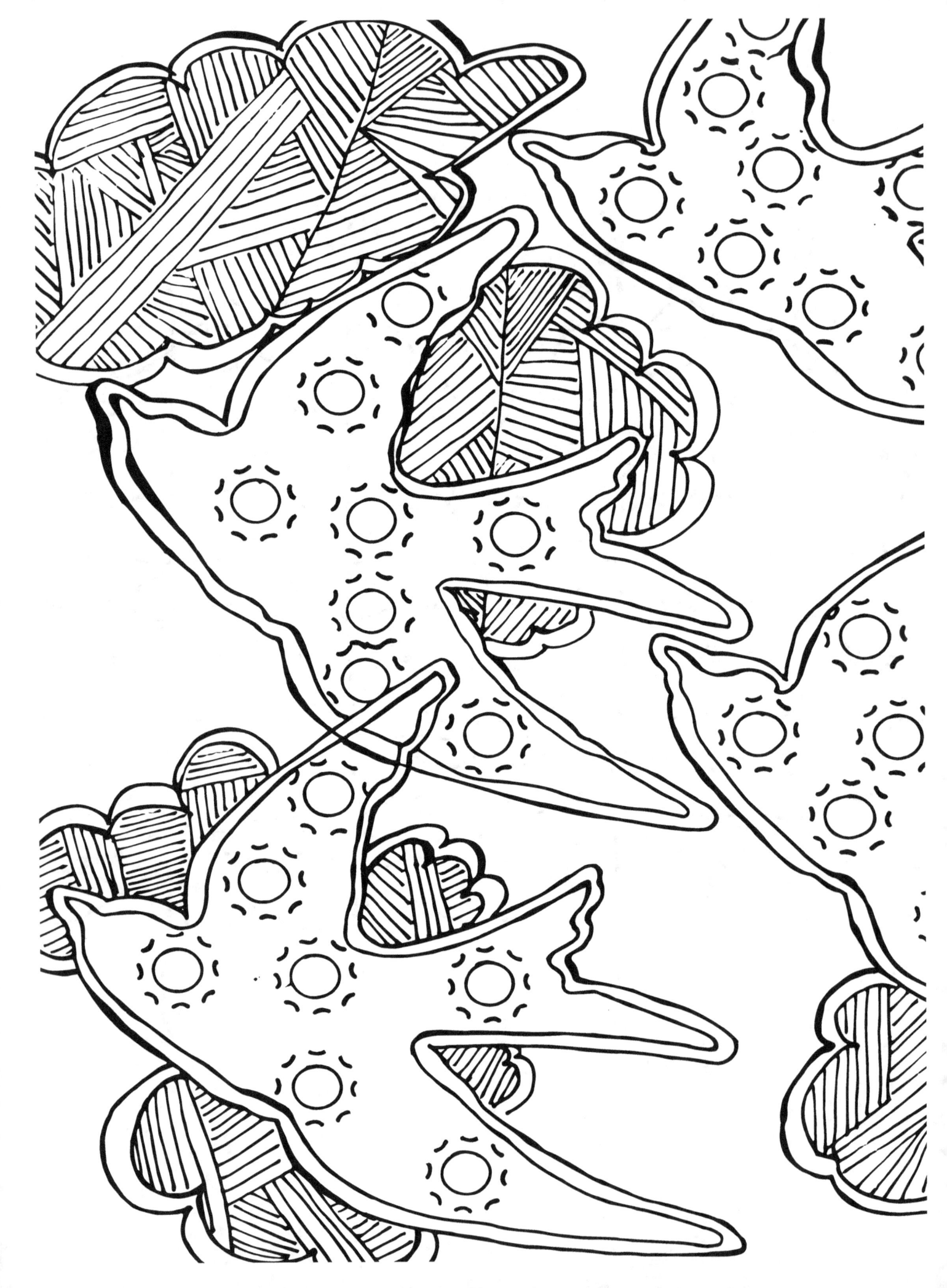

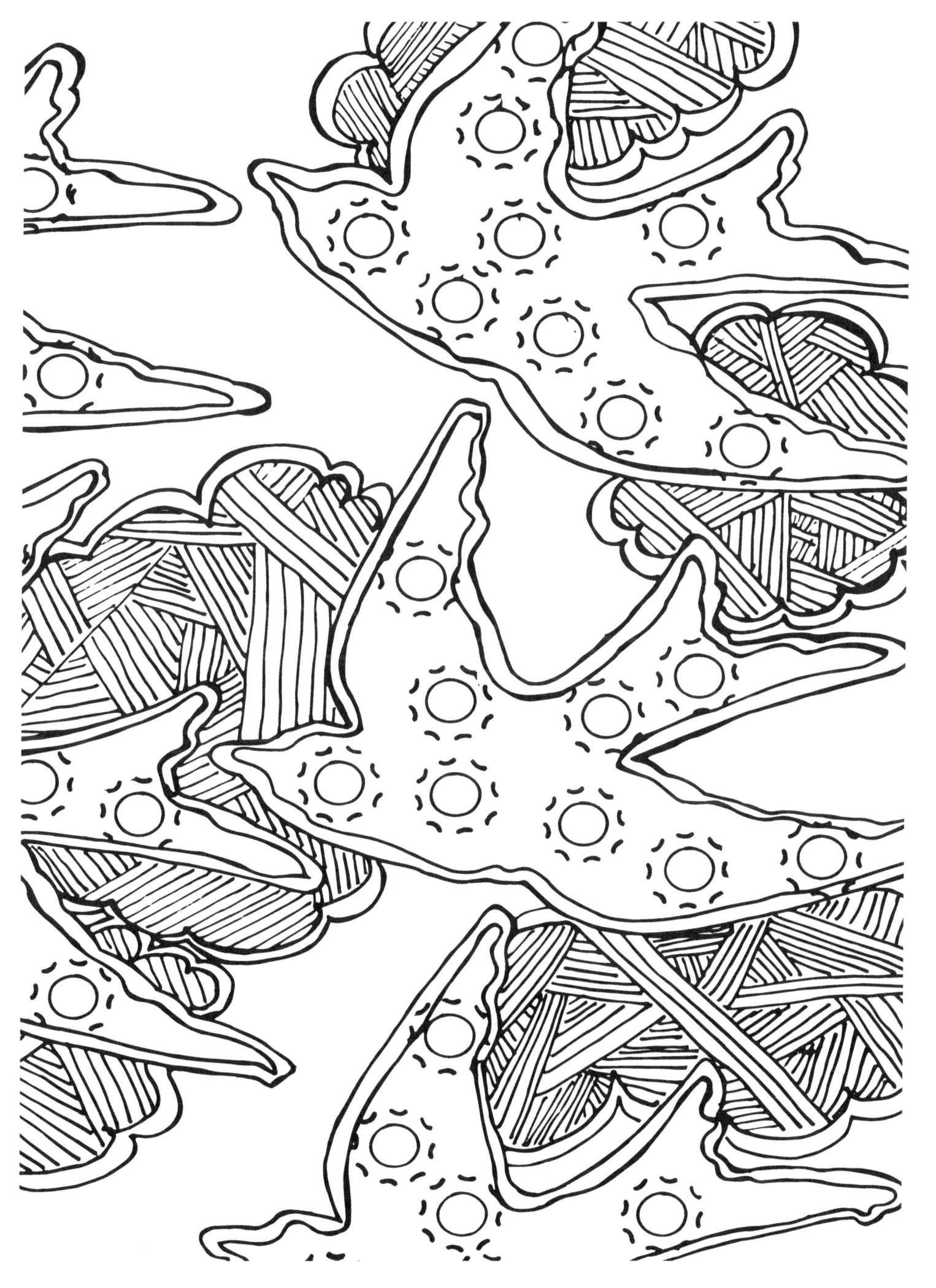

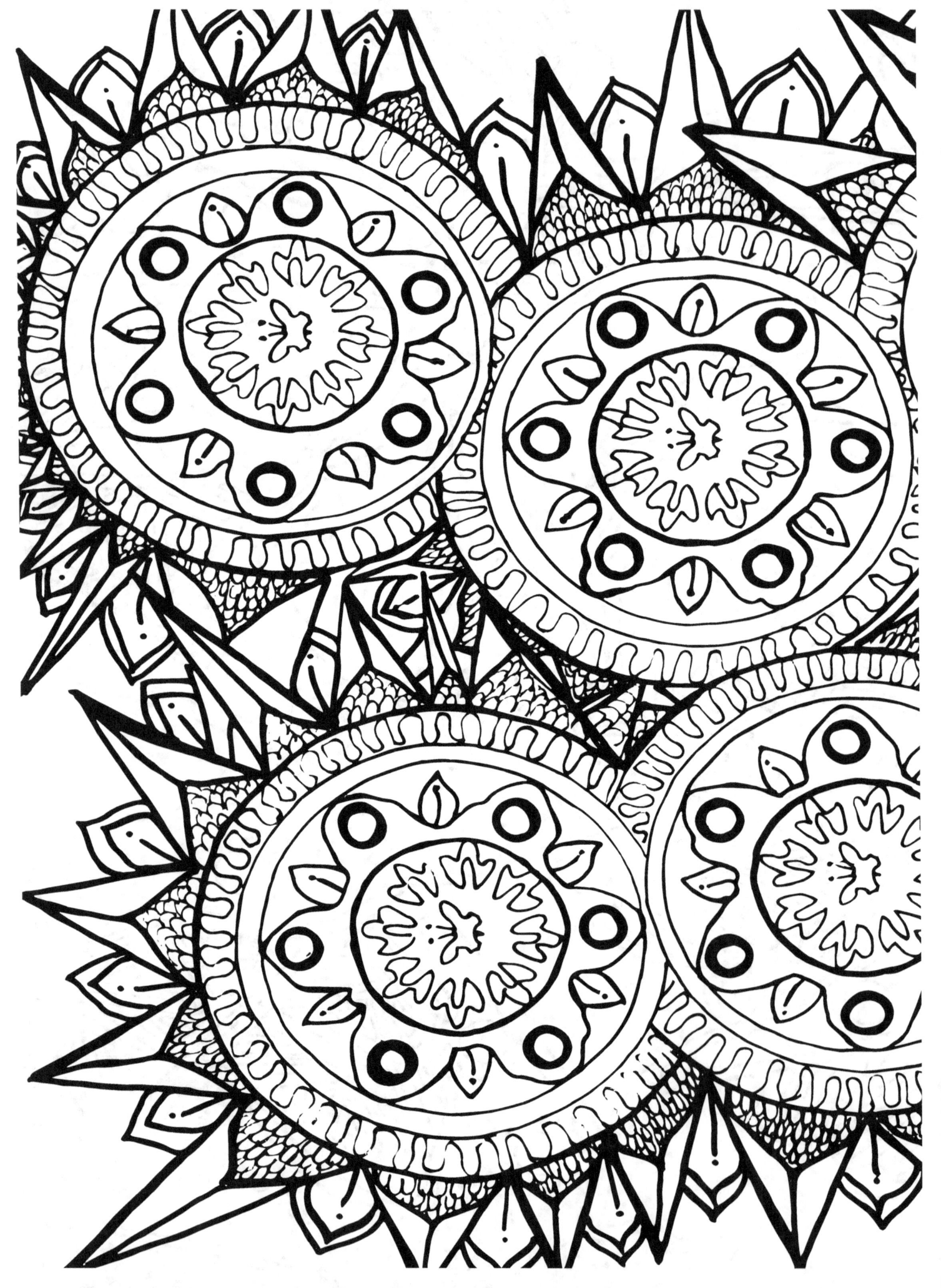

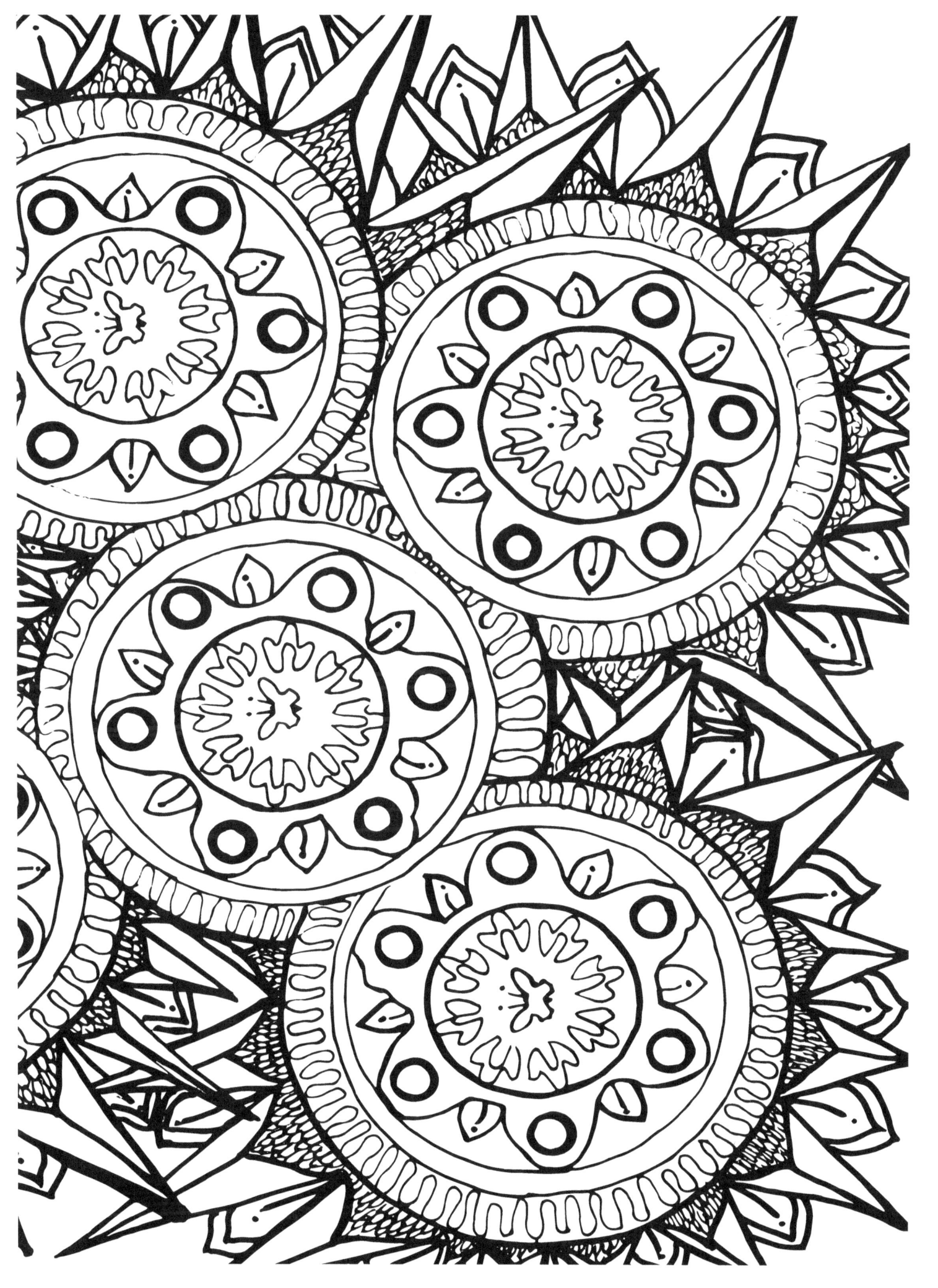

Hope in God, who richly provides us with everything for our enjoyment.

1 Tim 6:17

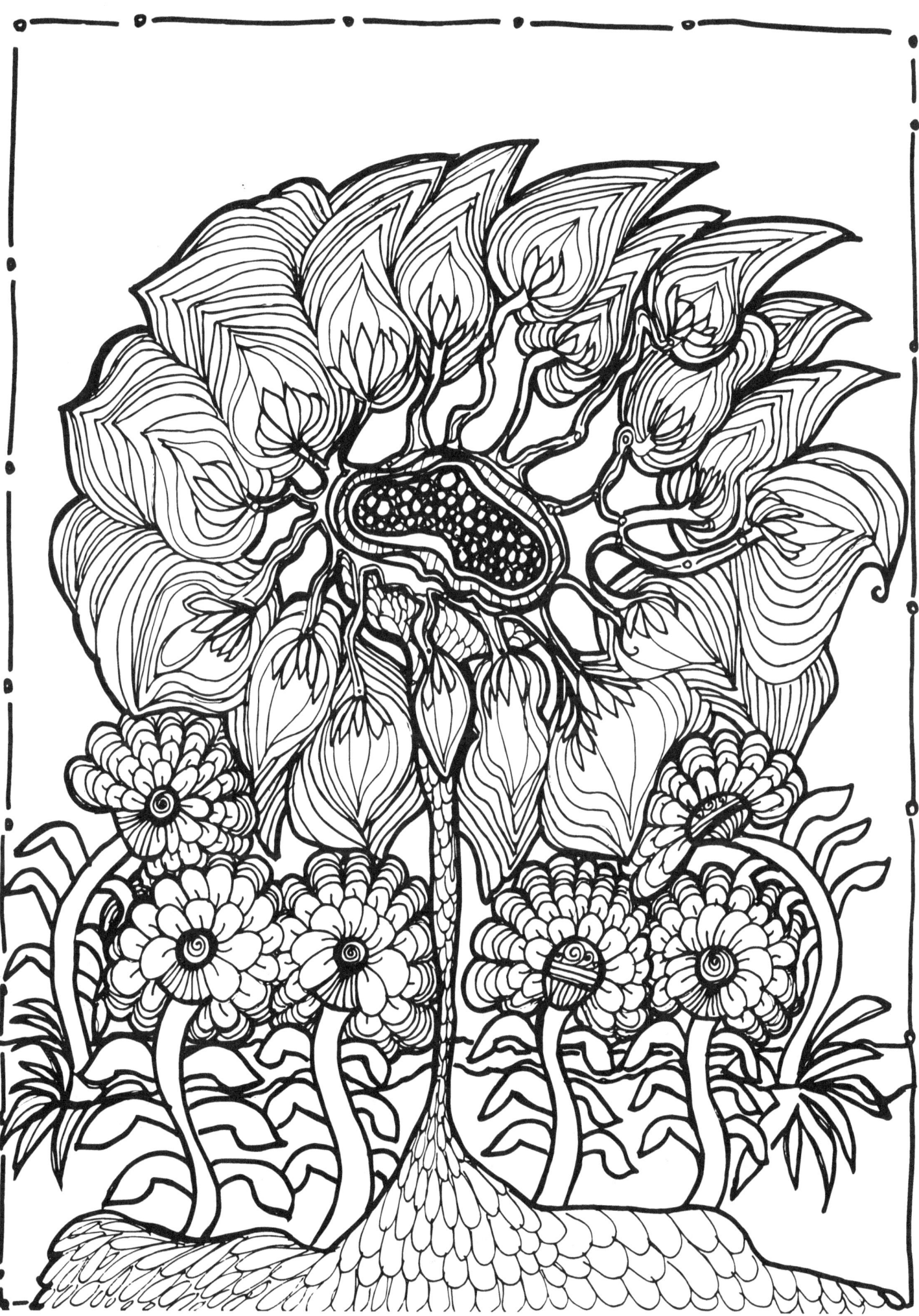

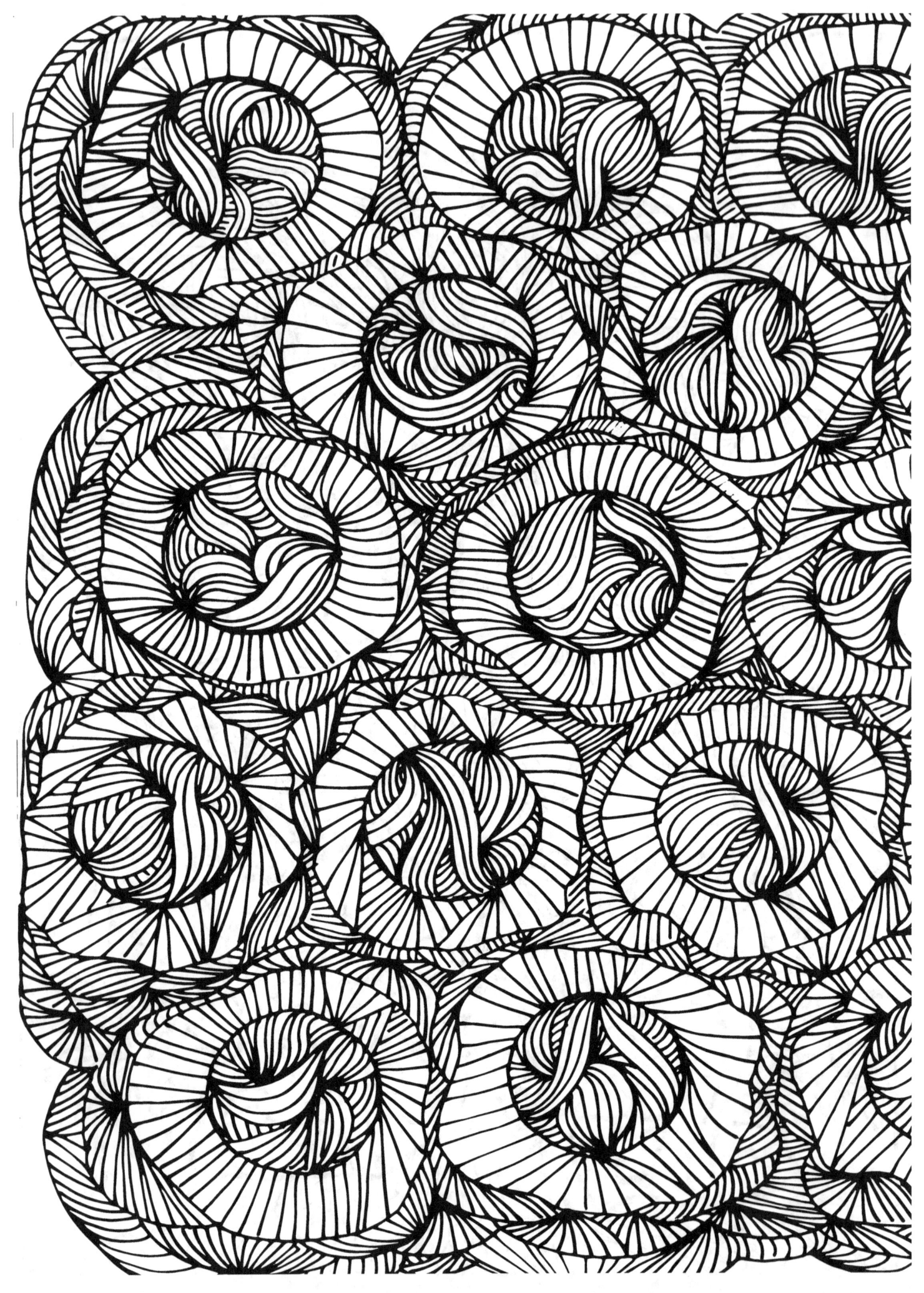

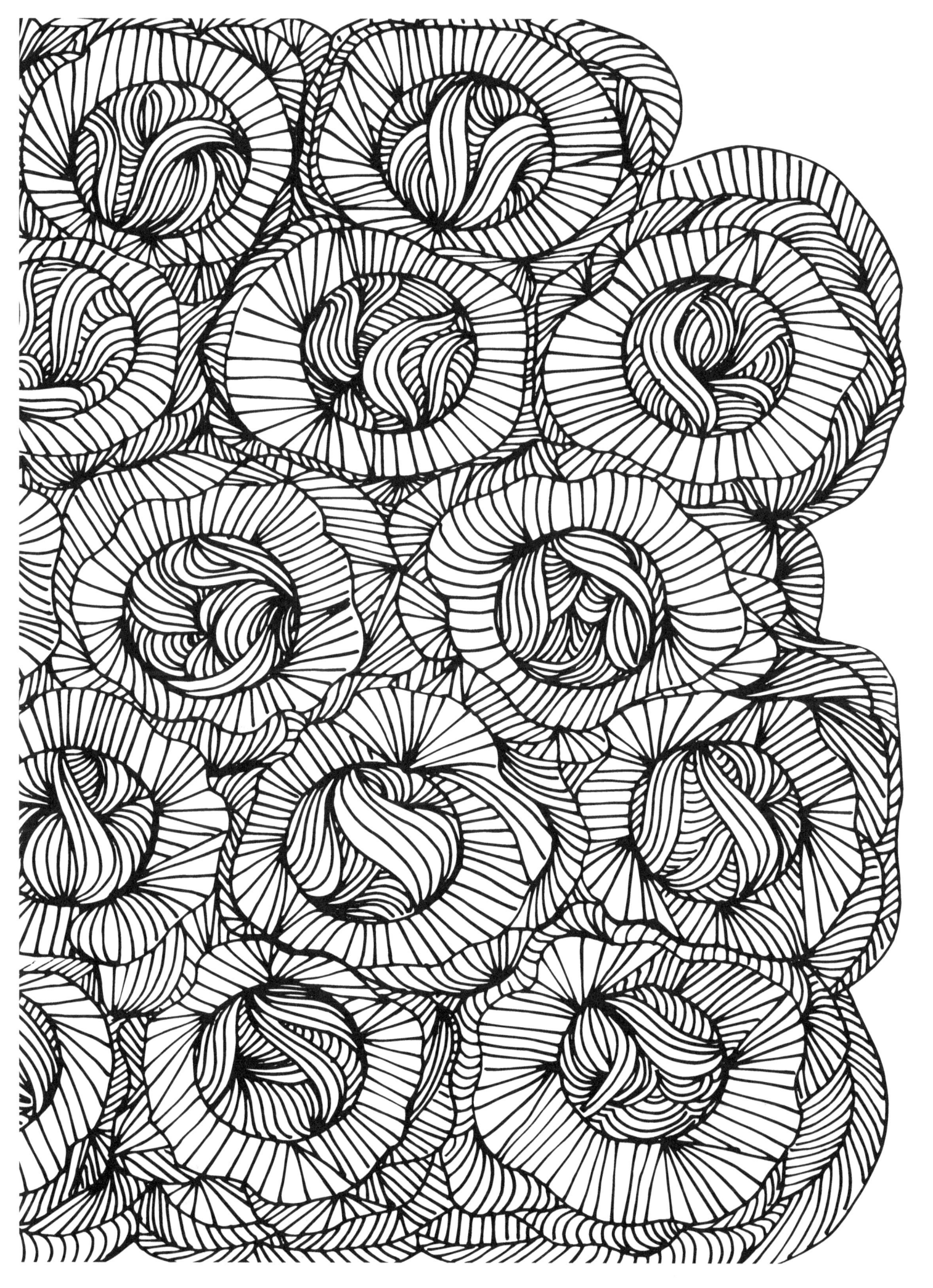

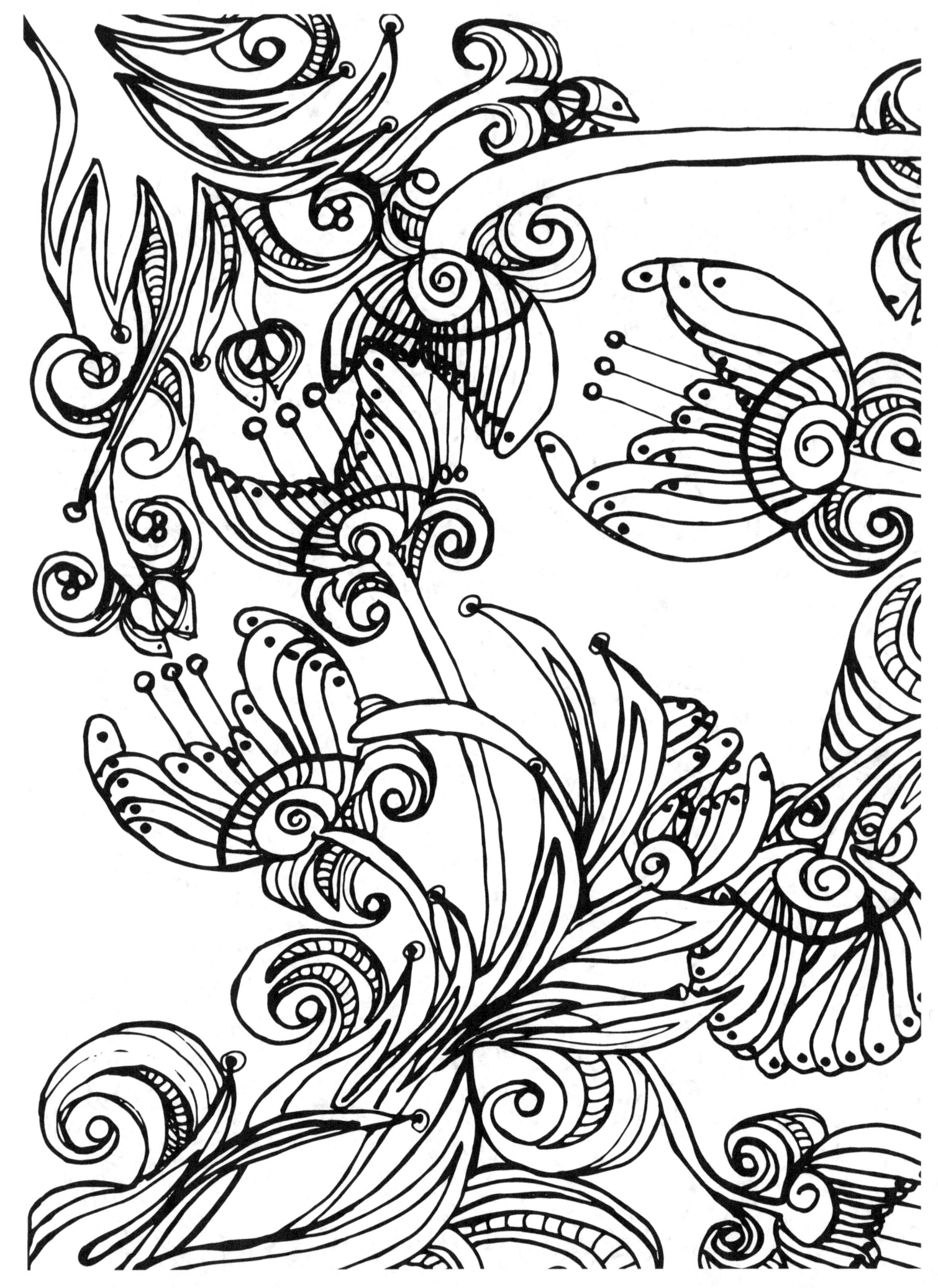

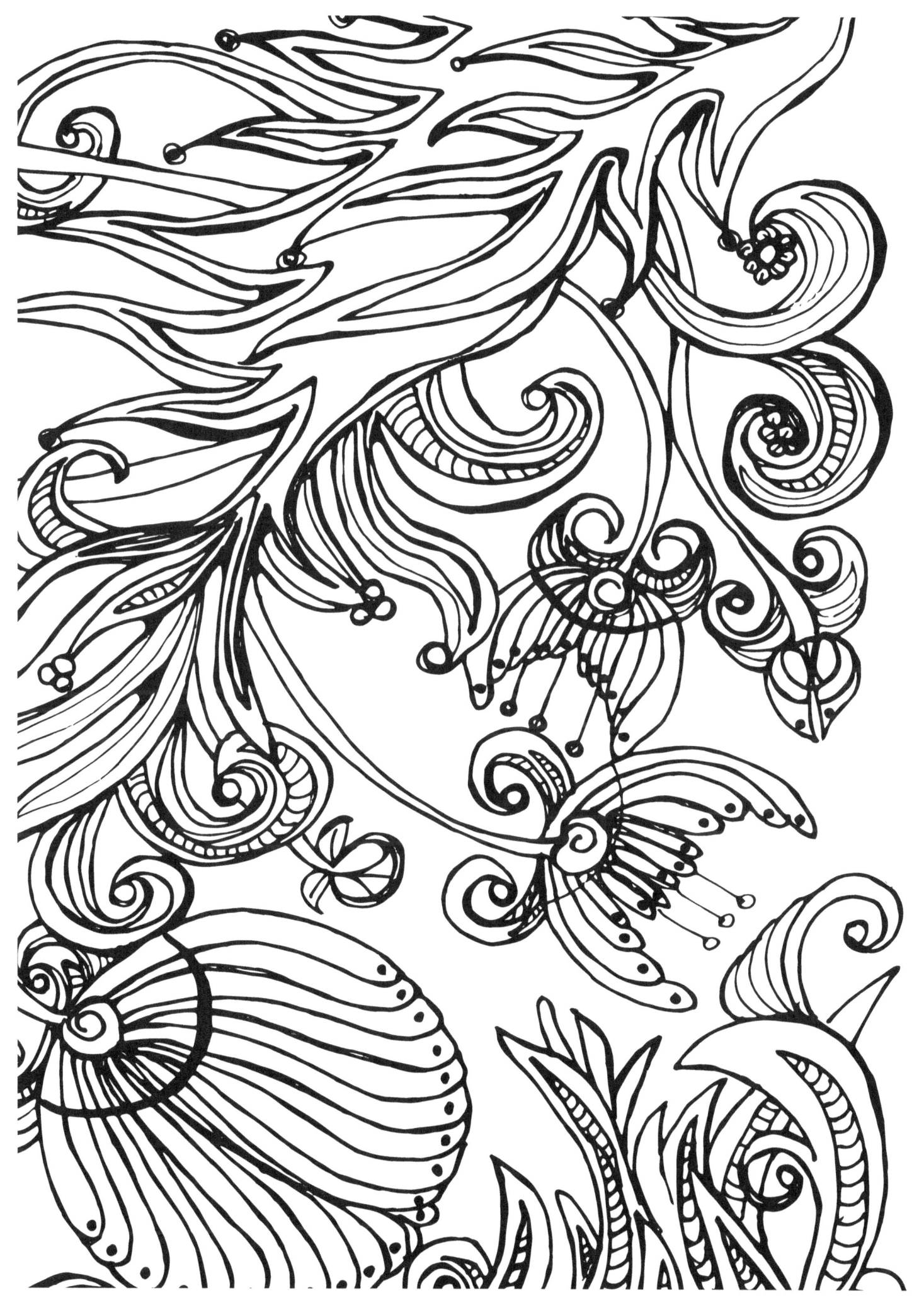

**Art enables us to find ourselves
and lose ourselves at the same time.**

Thomas Merton

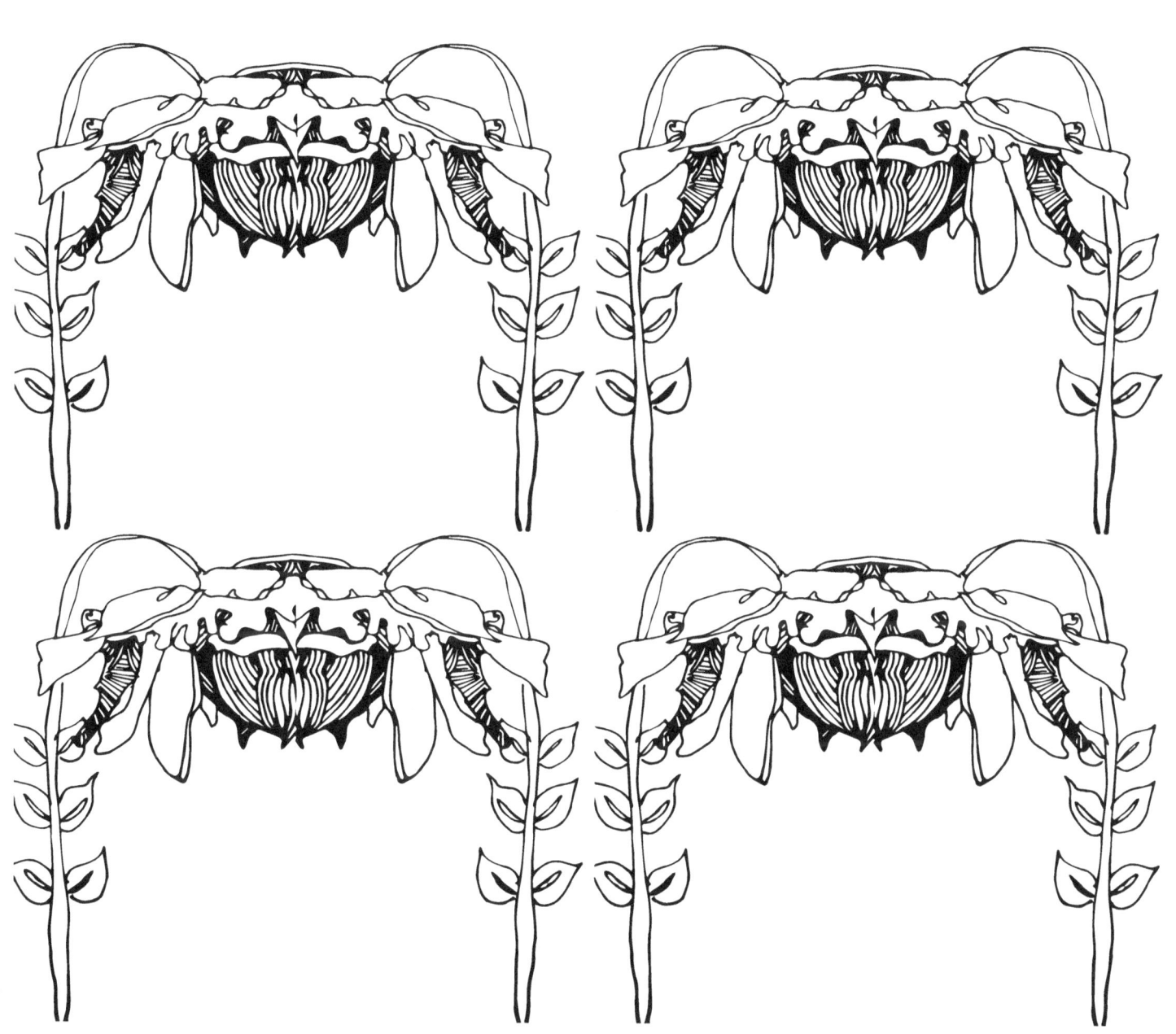

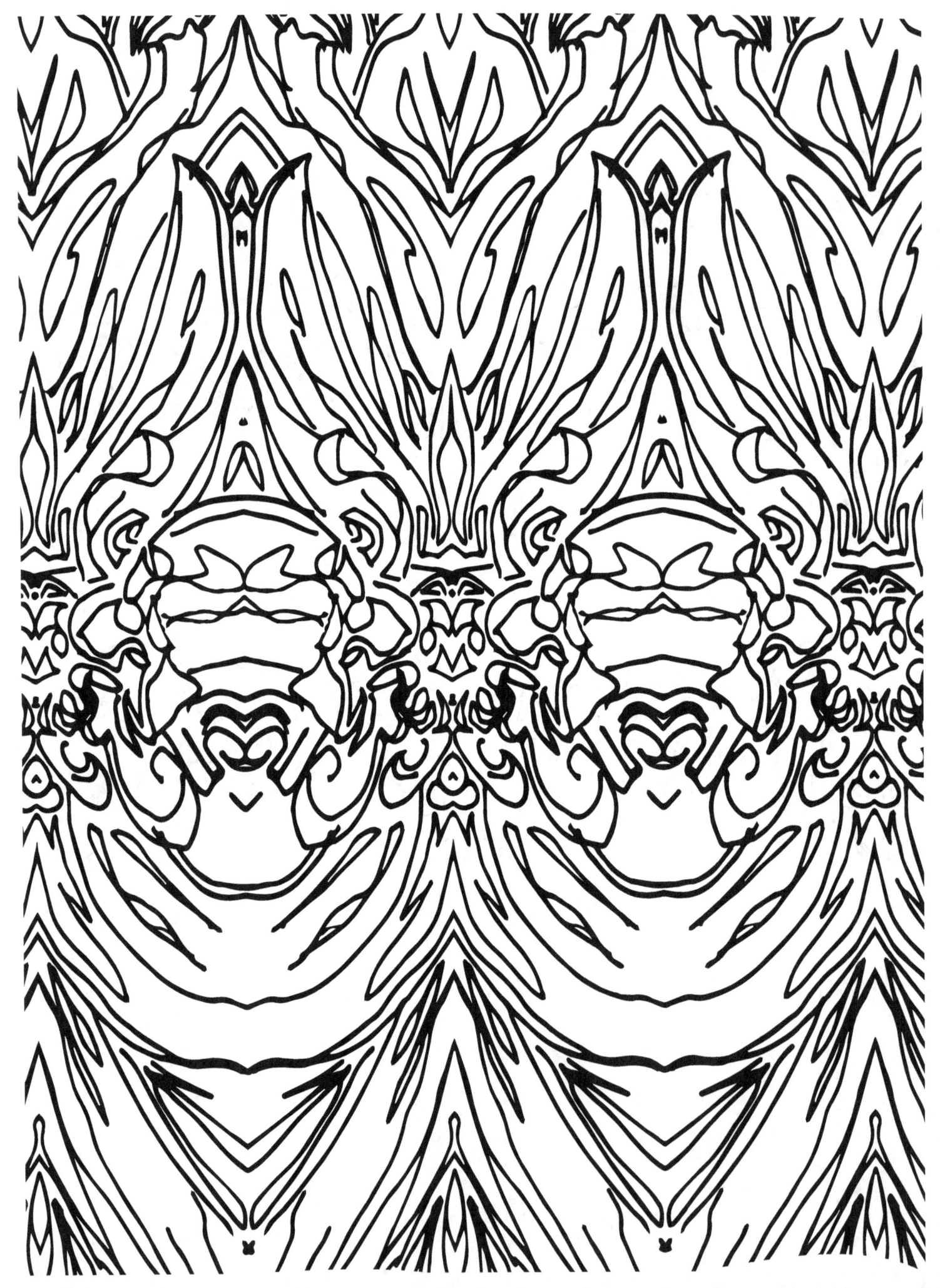

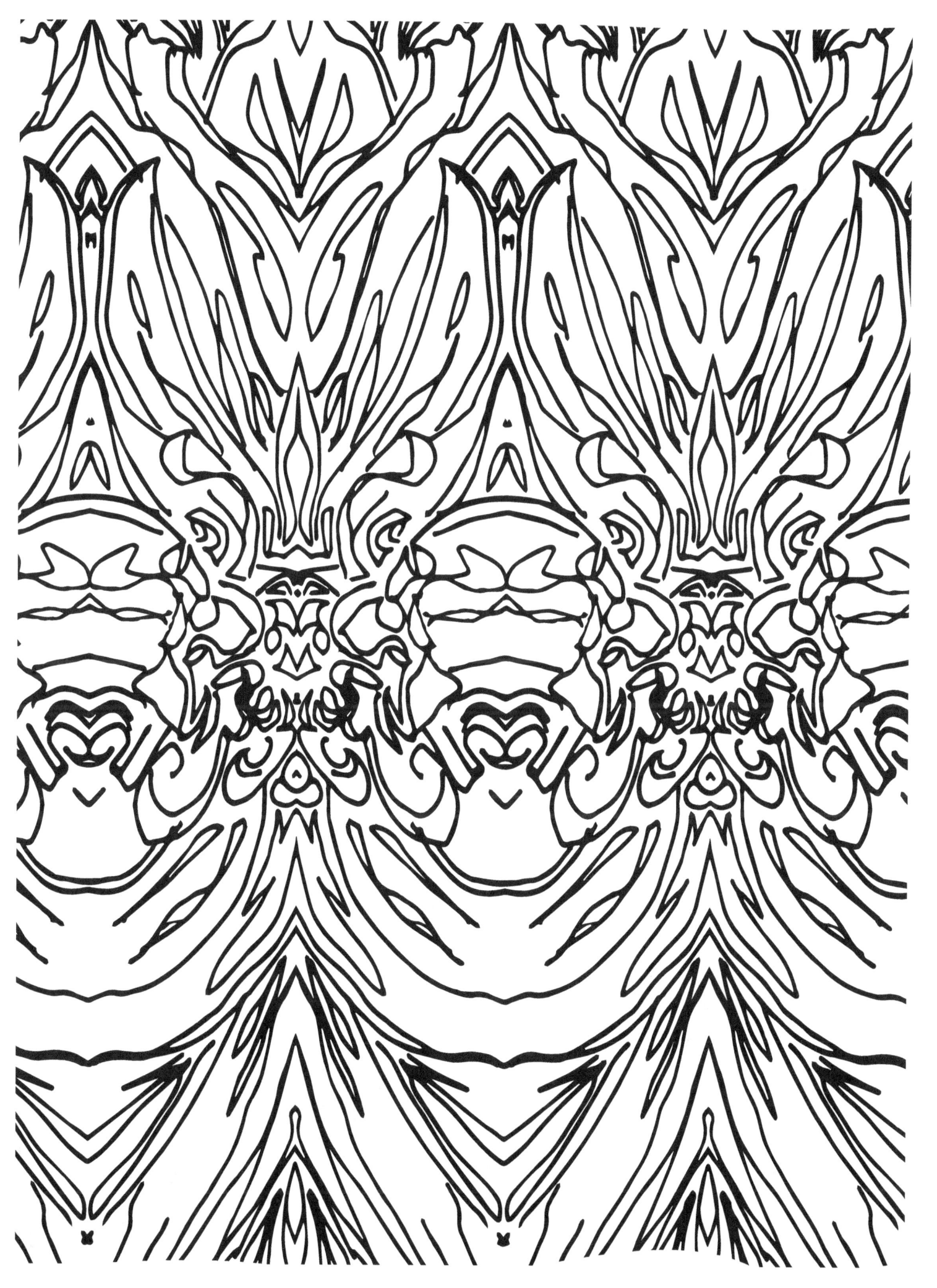

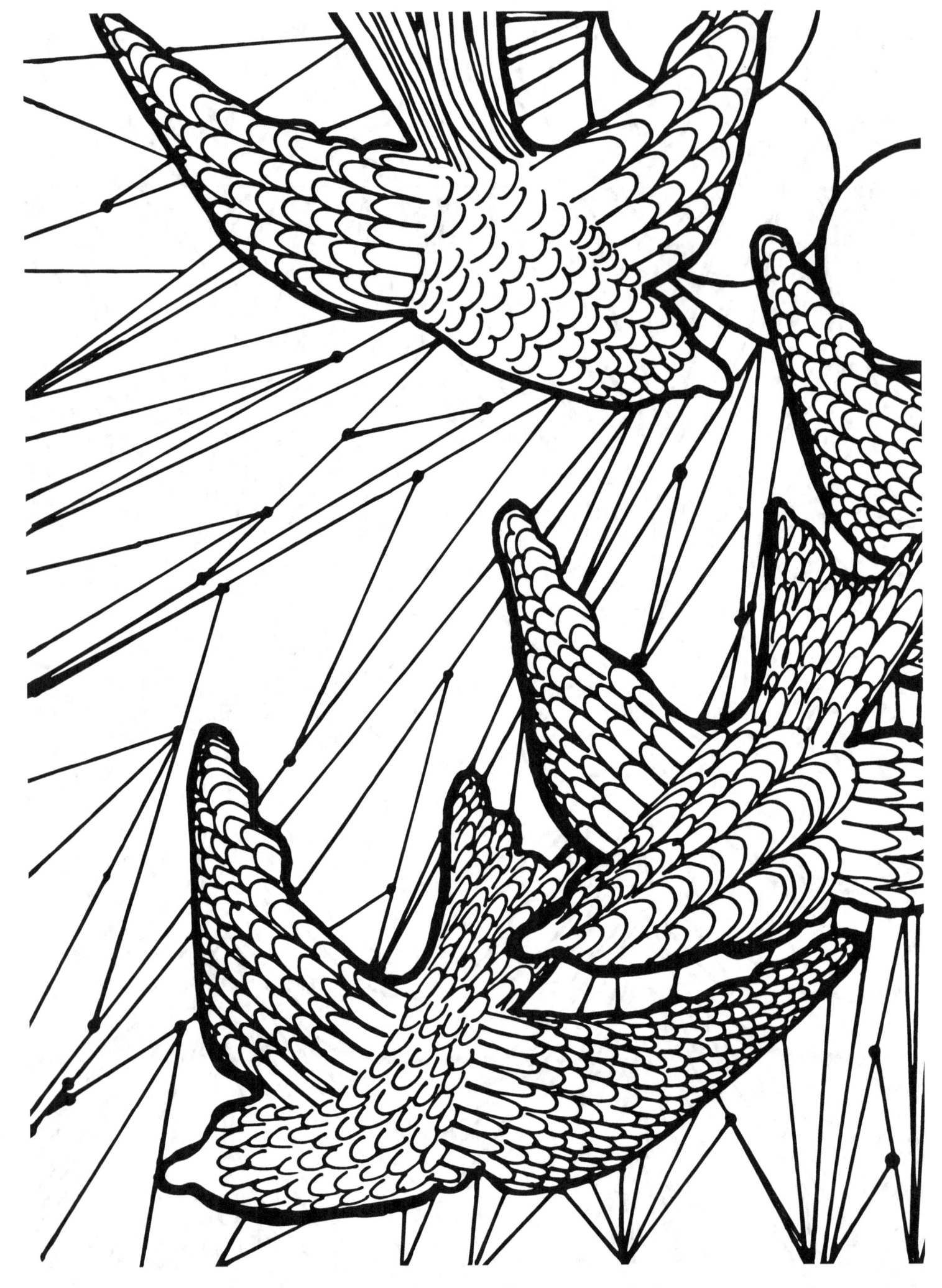

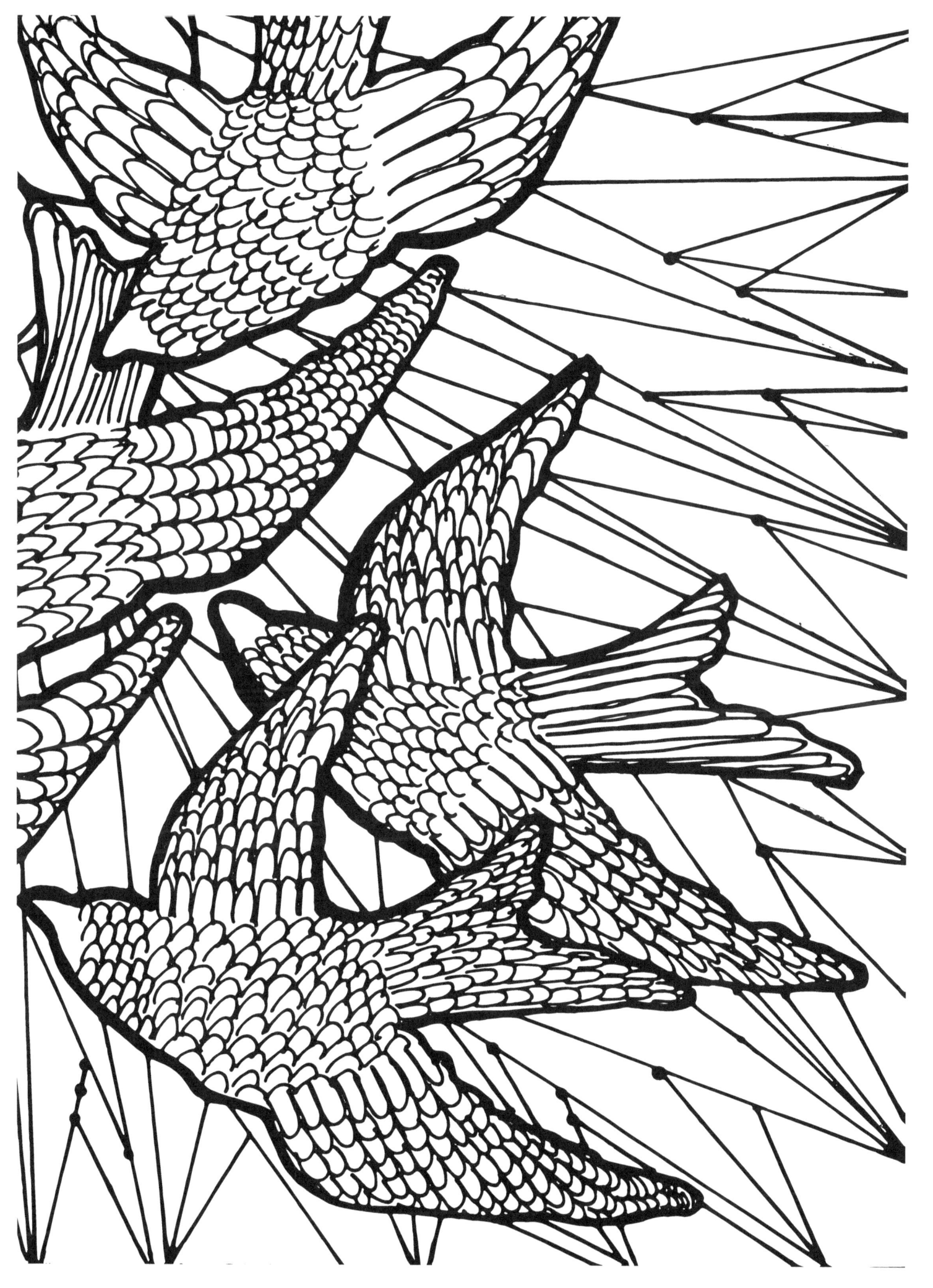

In a picture I want to say something comforting.

Vincent Van Gogh

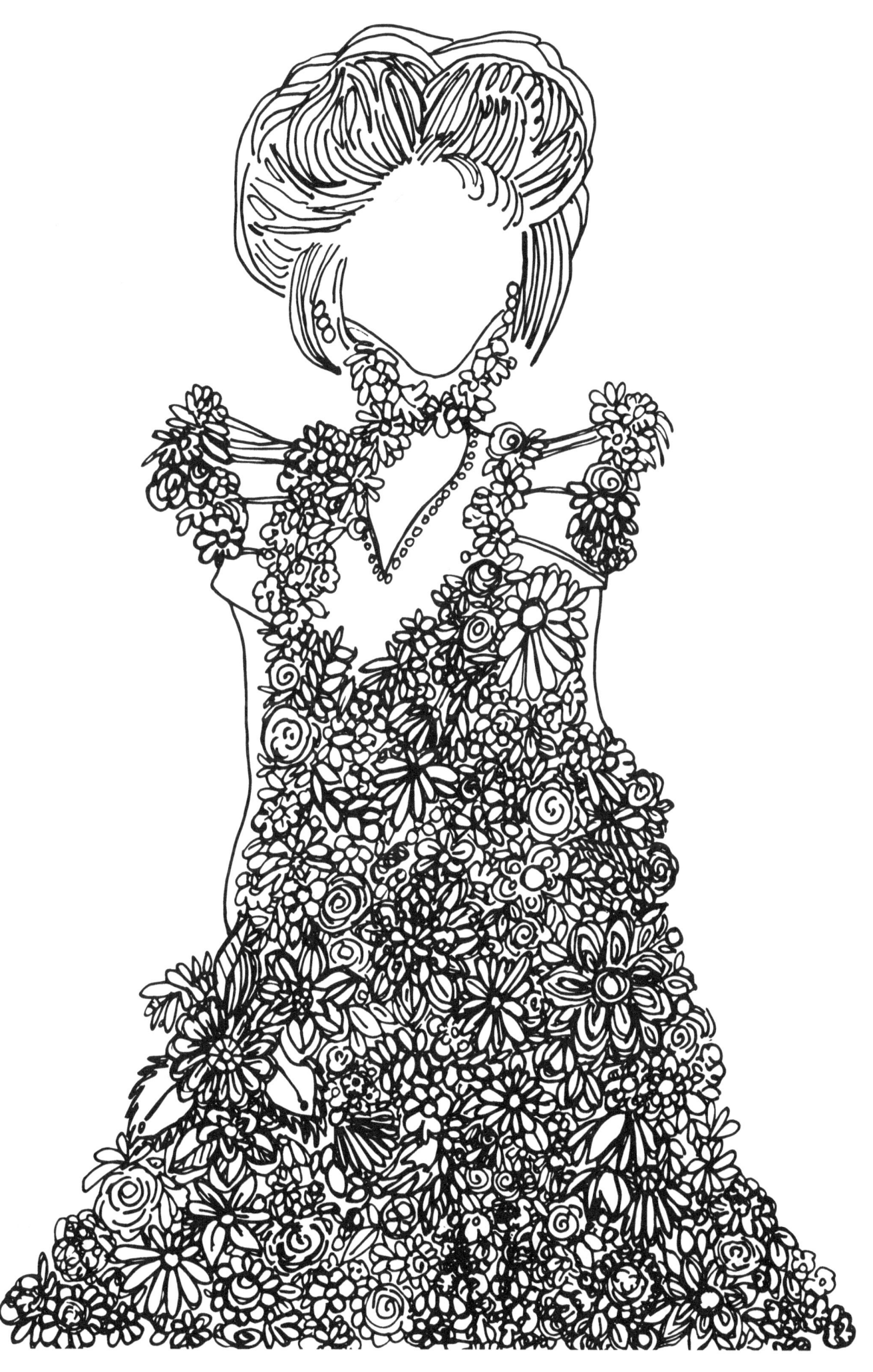

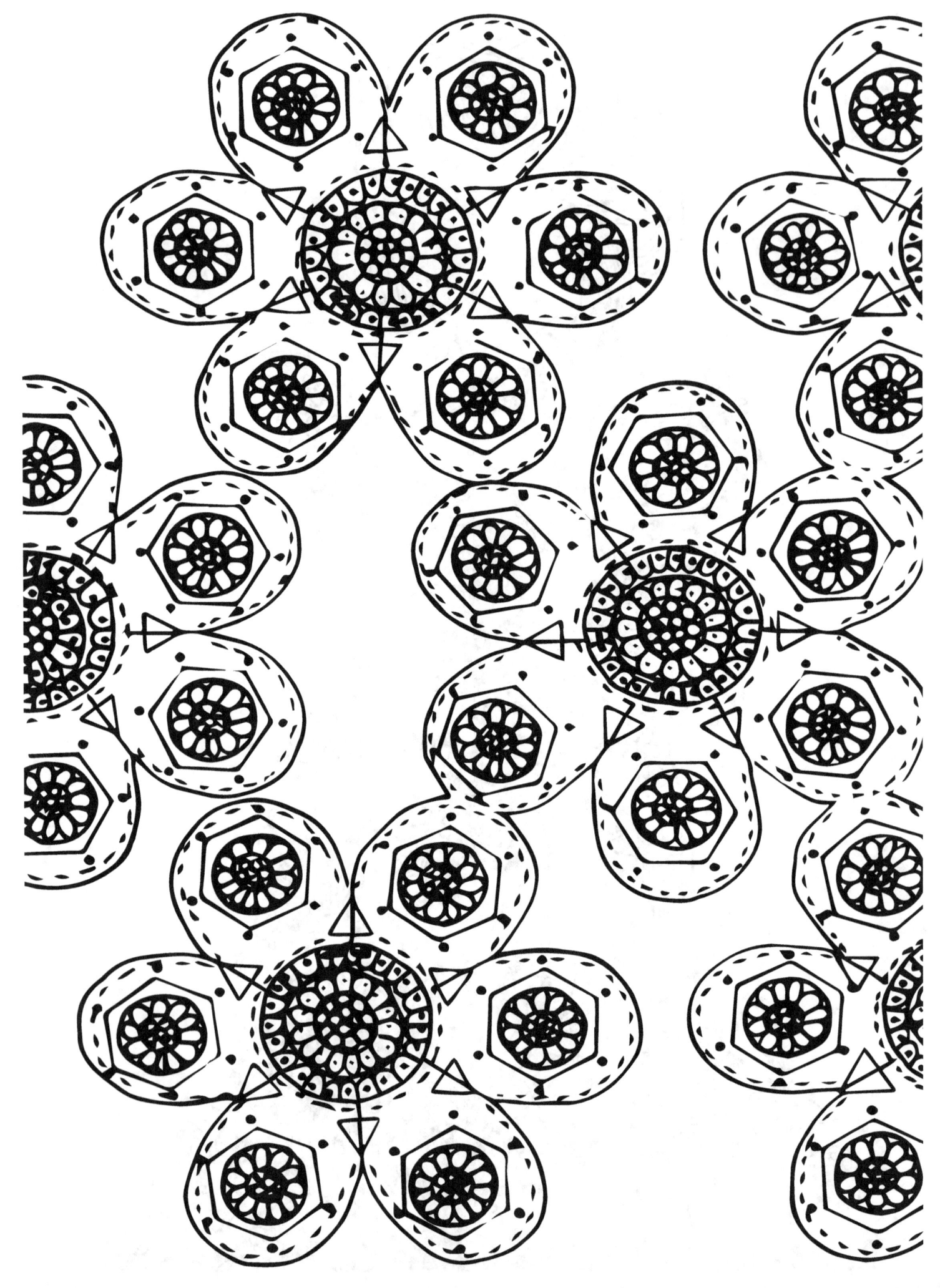

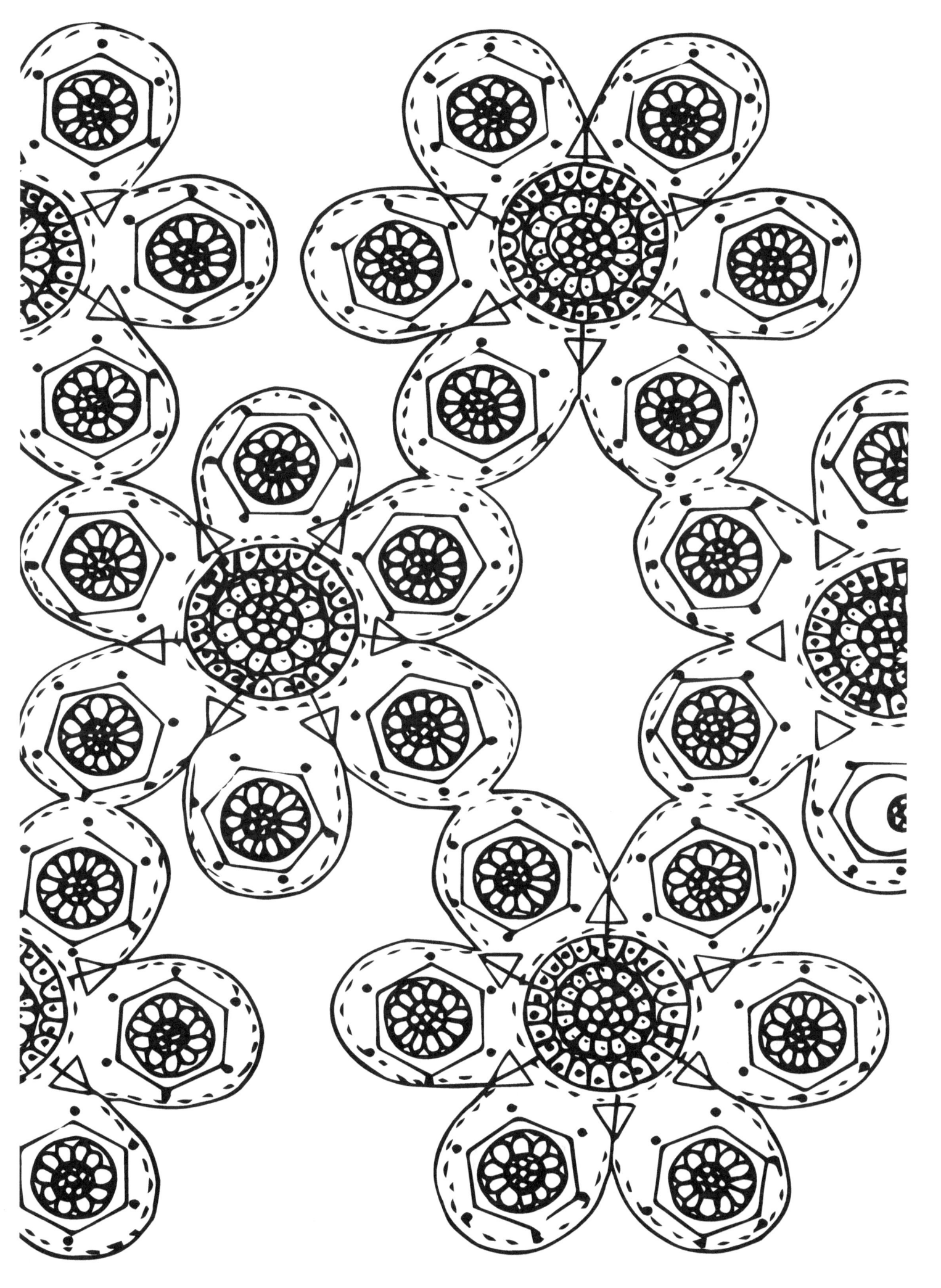

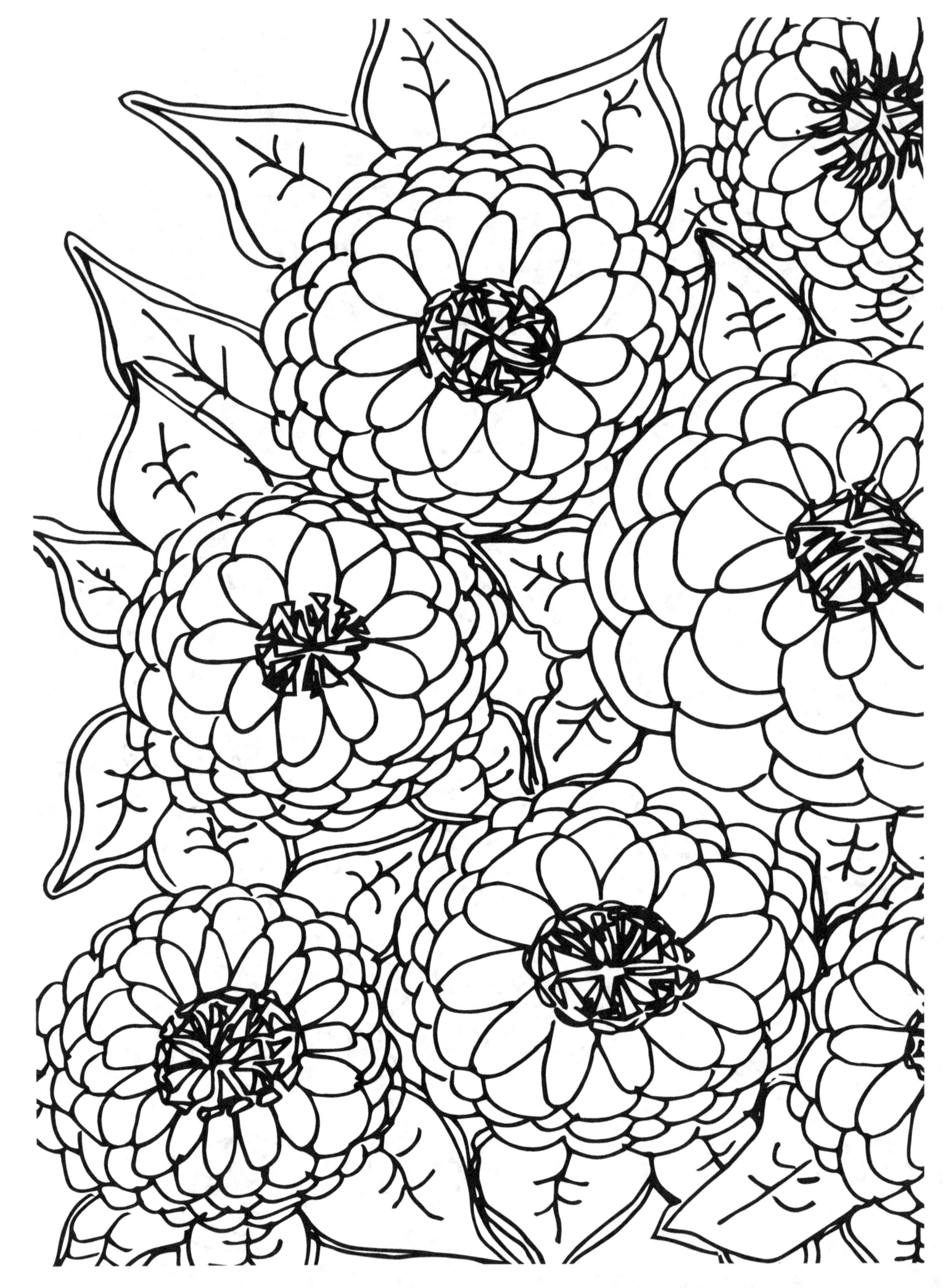

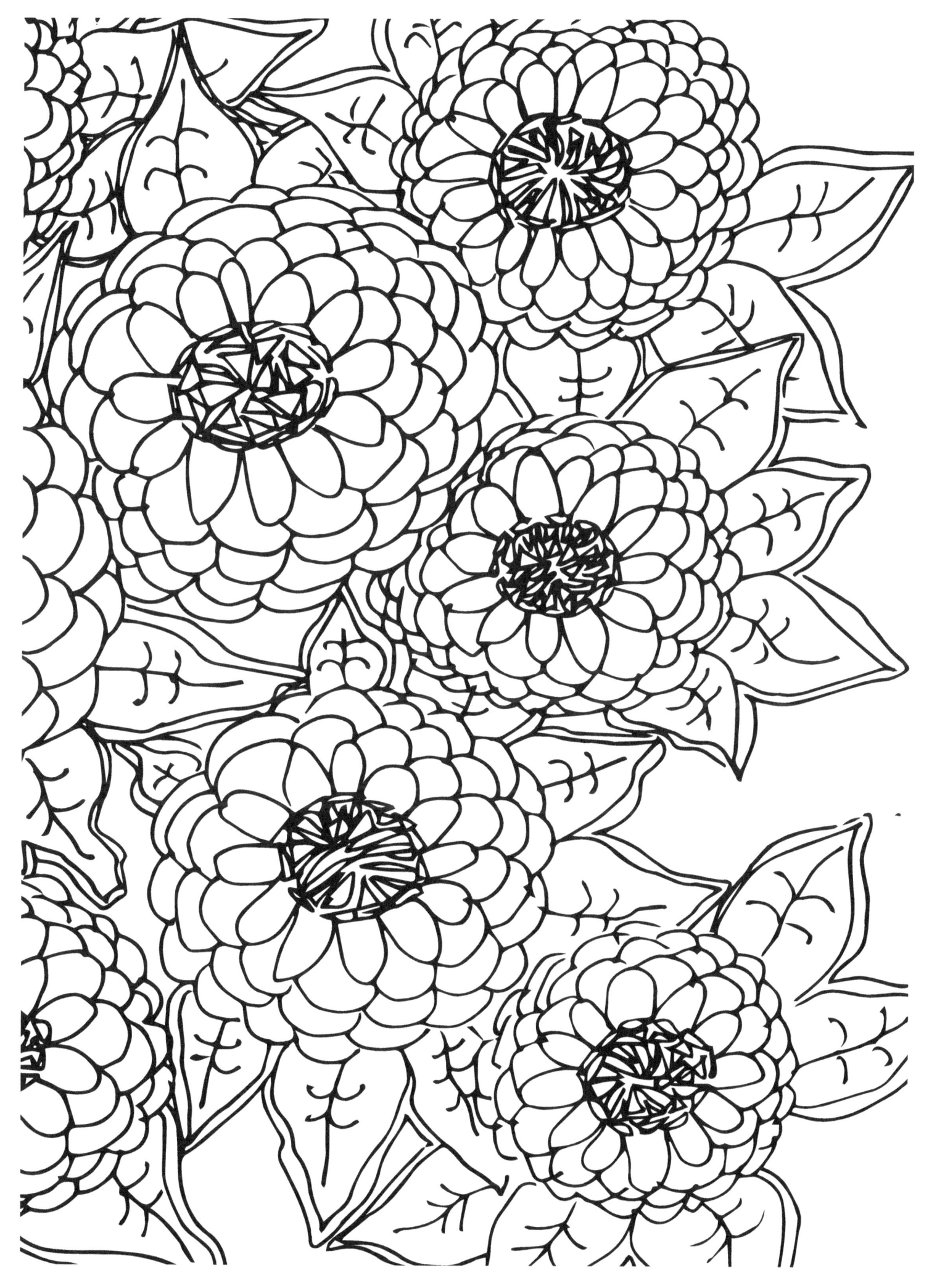

Creativity is not a competition.

Autumn Sky Hall

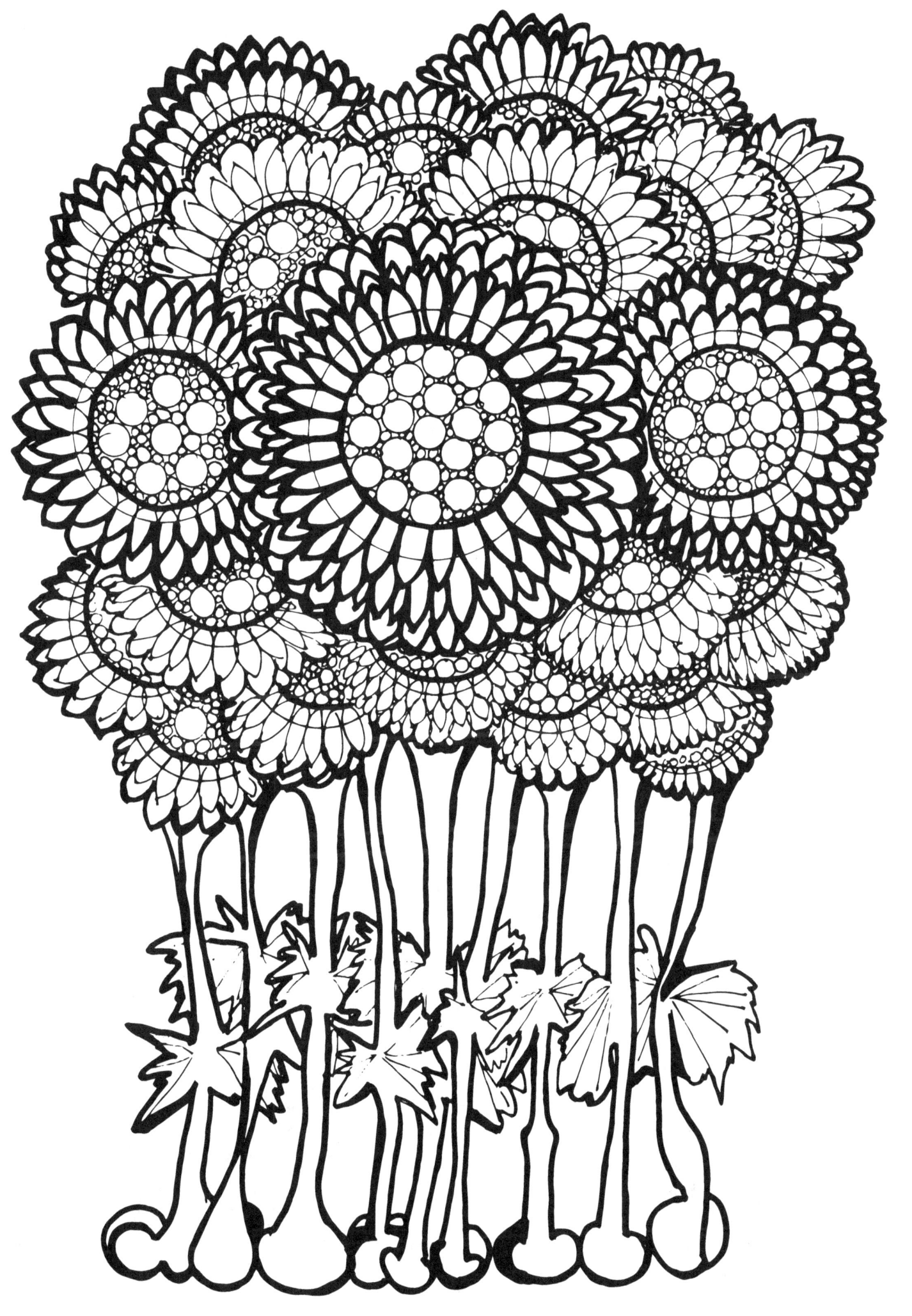

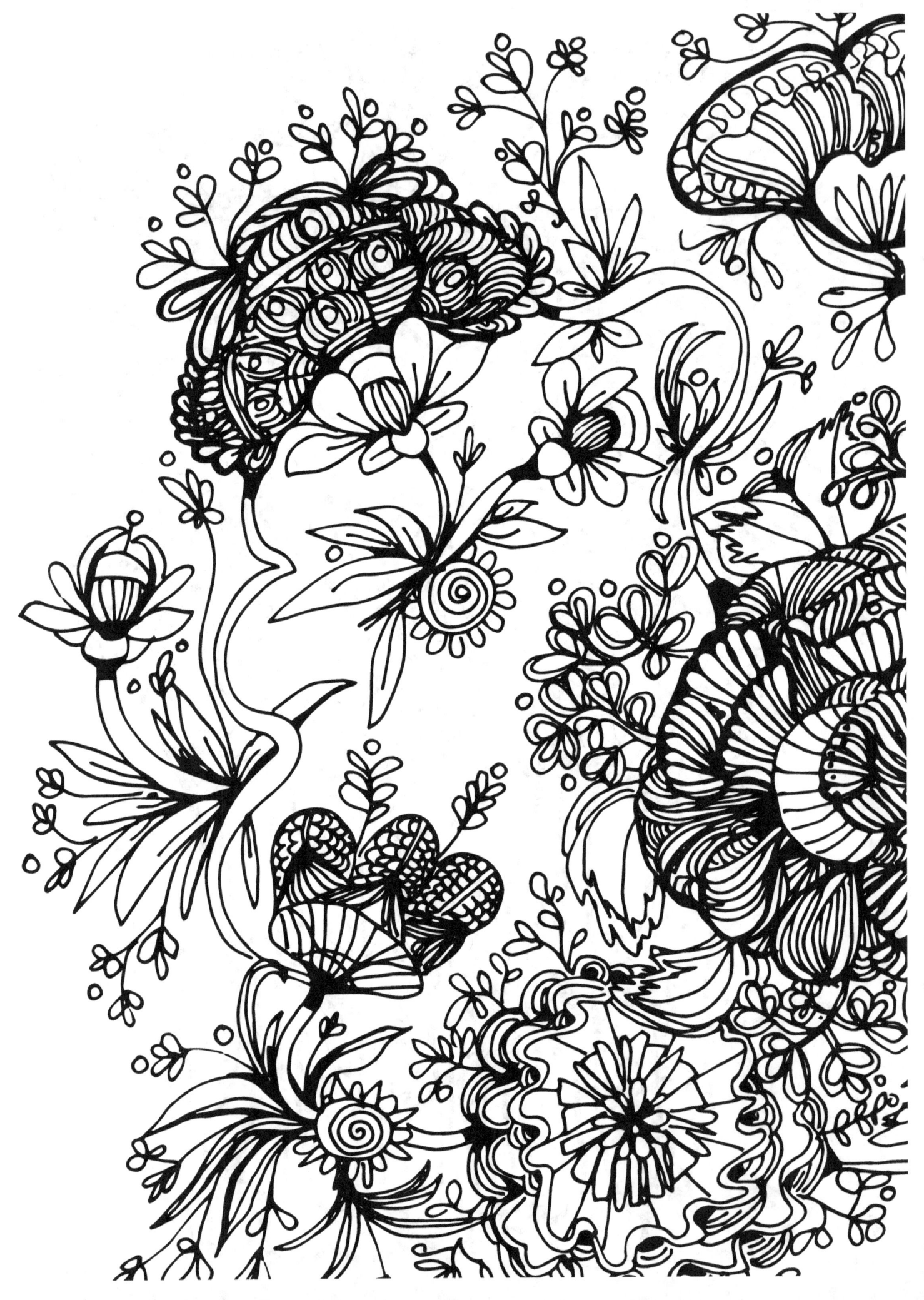

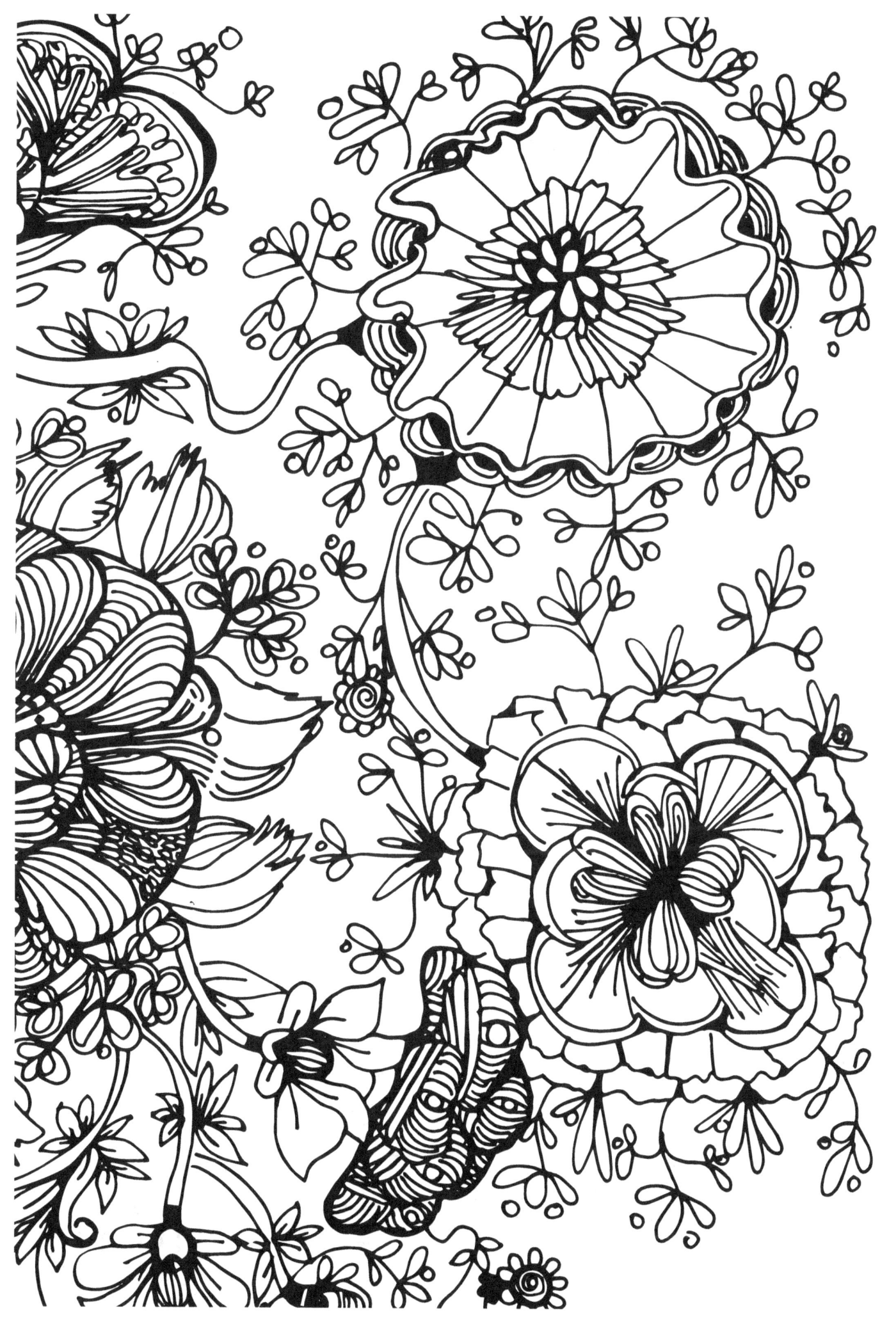

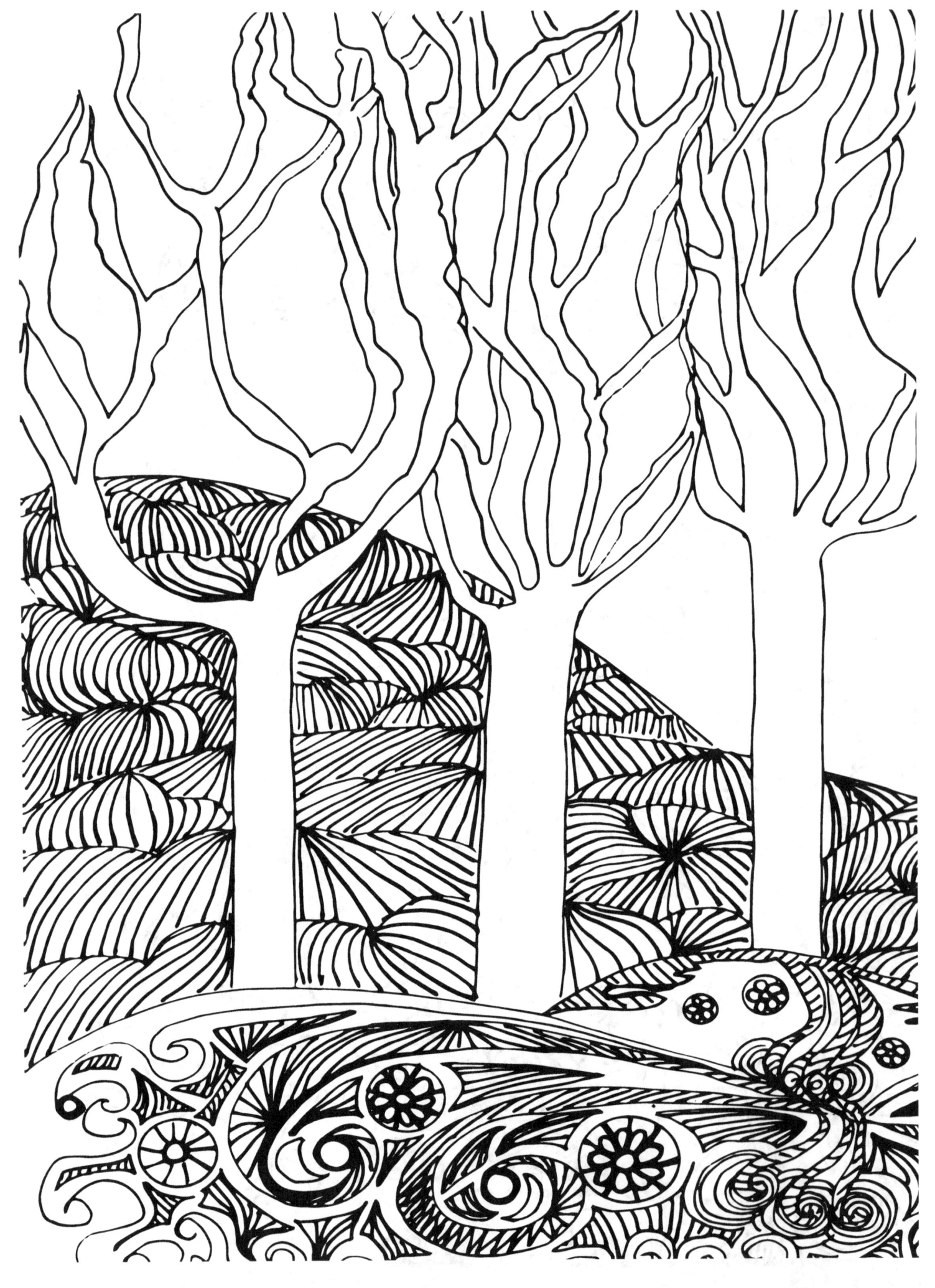

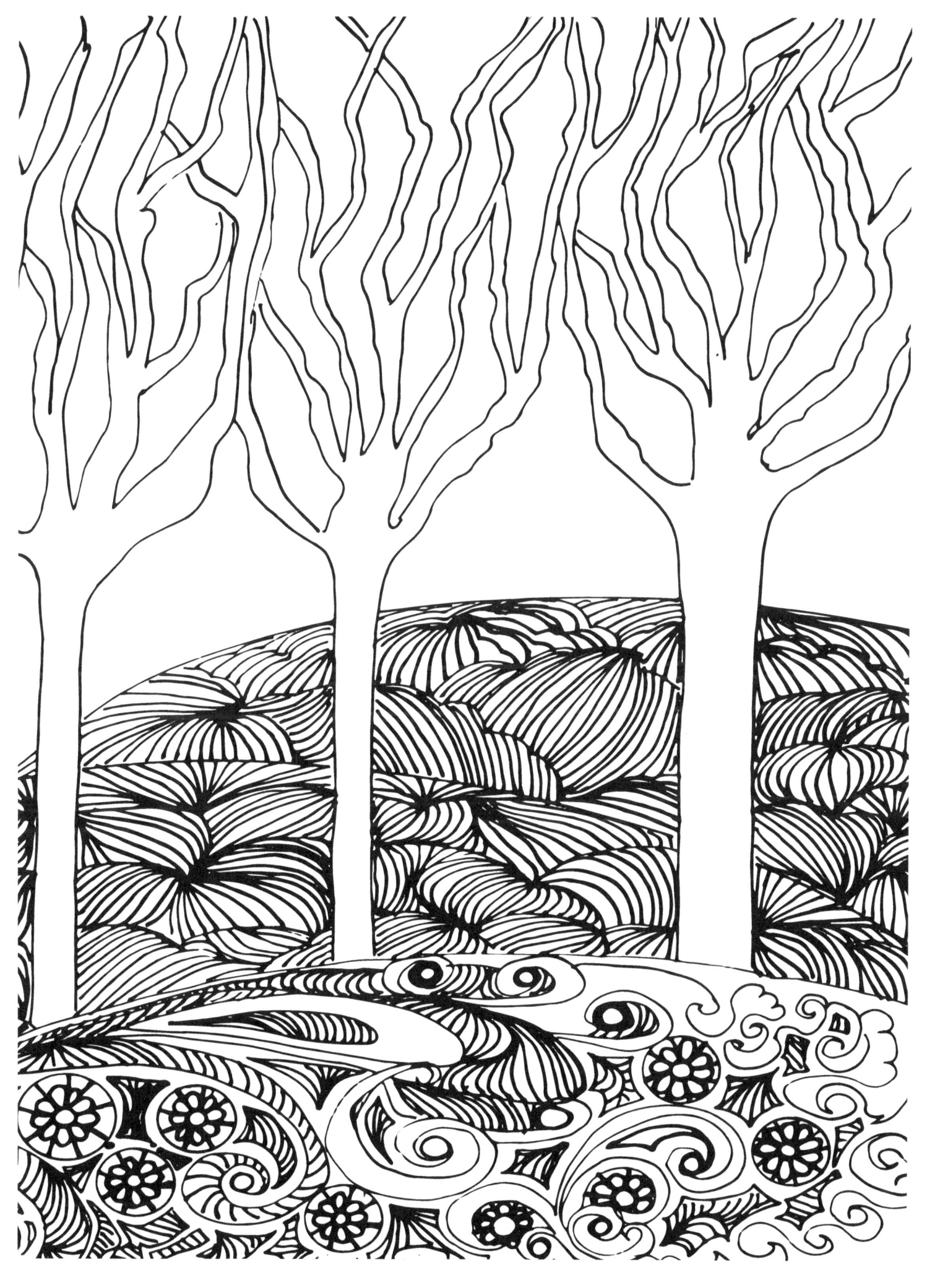

Every artist dips his brush in his own soul, and paints his own nature into his pictures.

Henry Ward Beecher

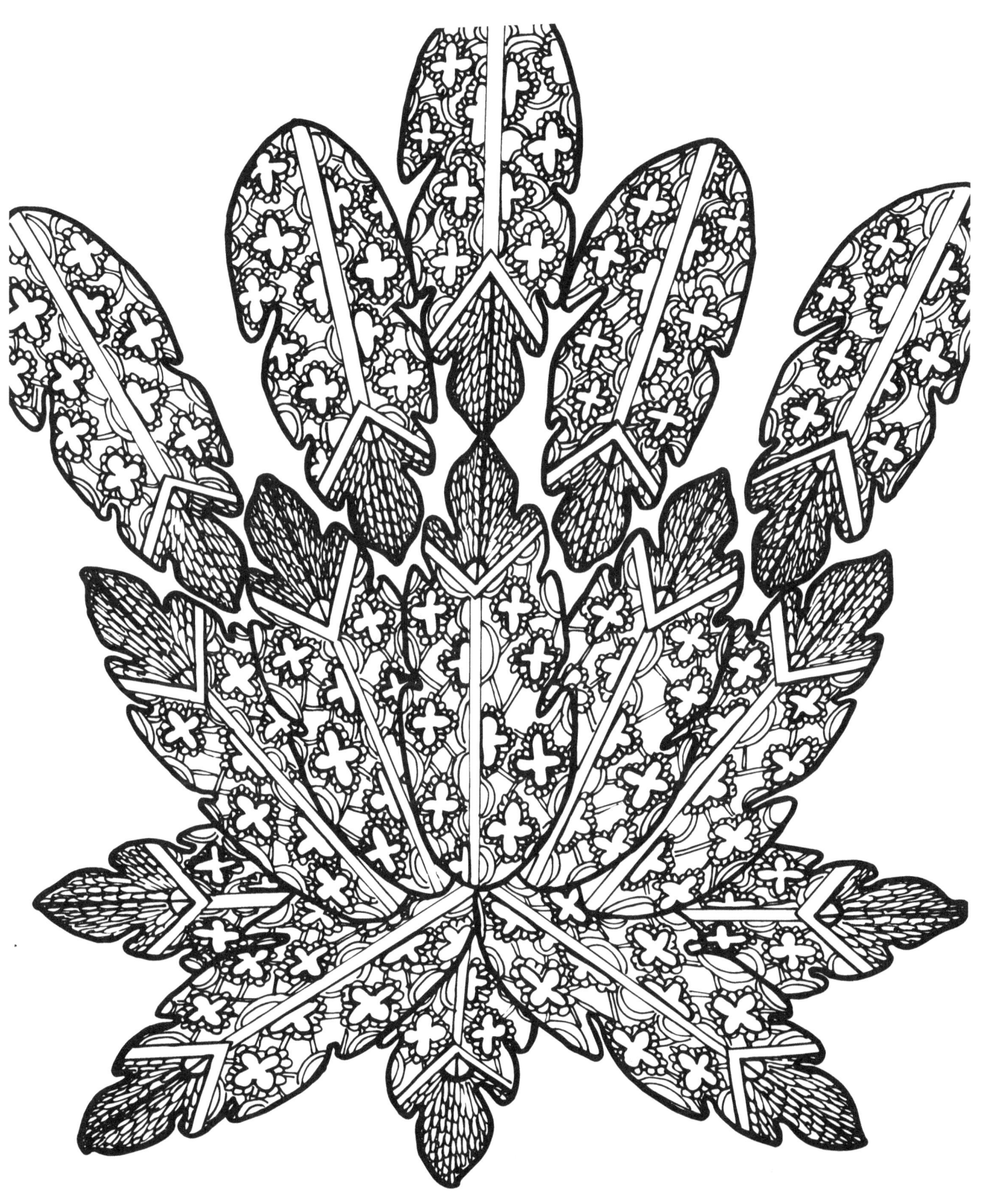

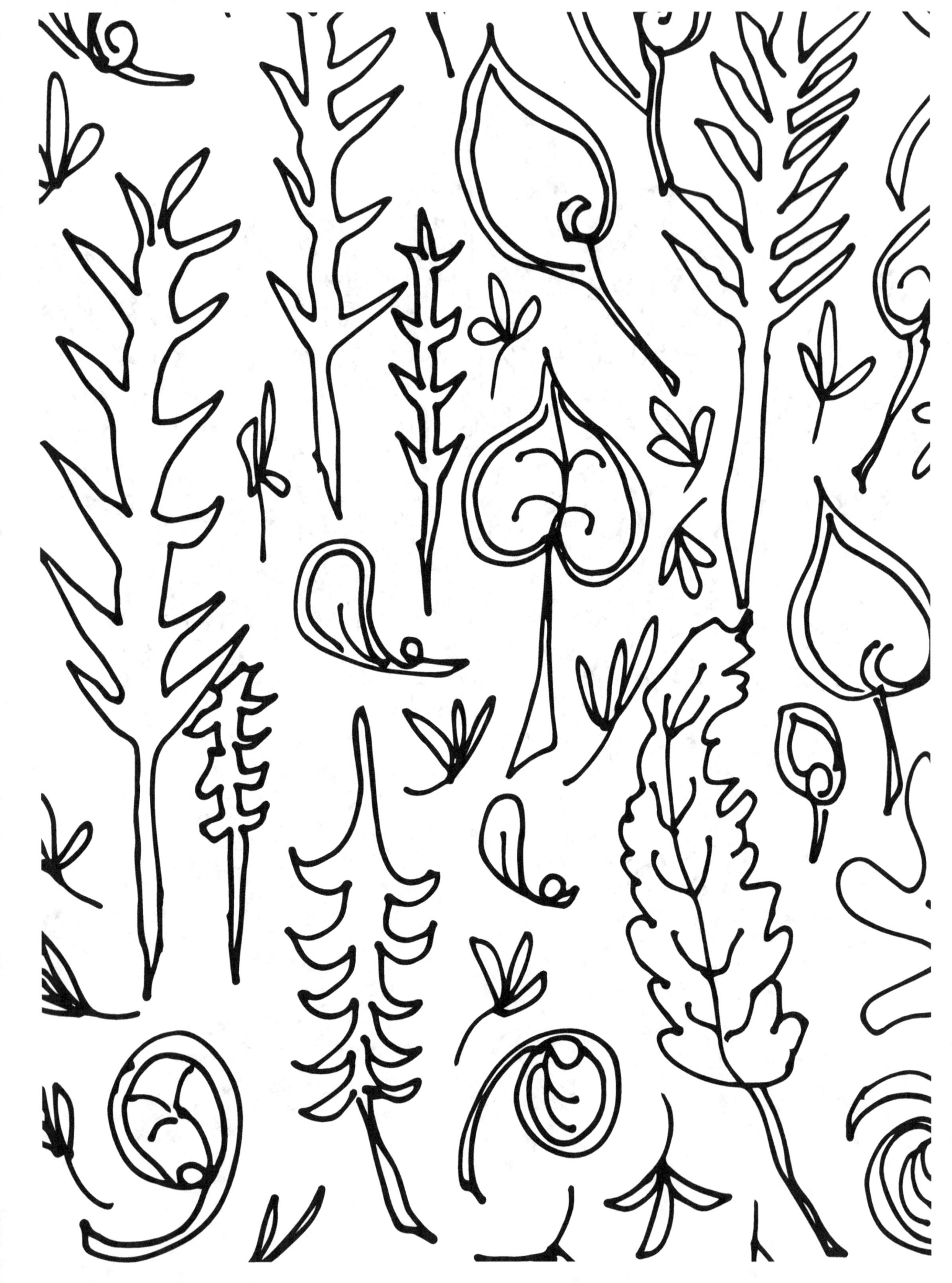

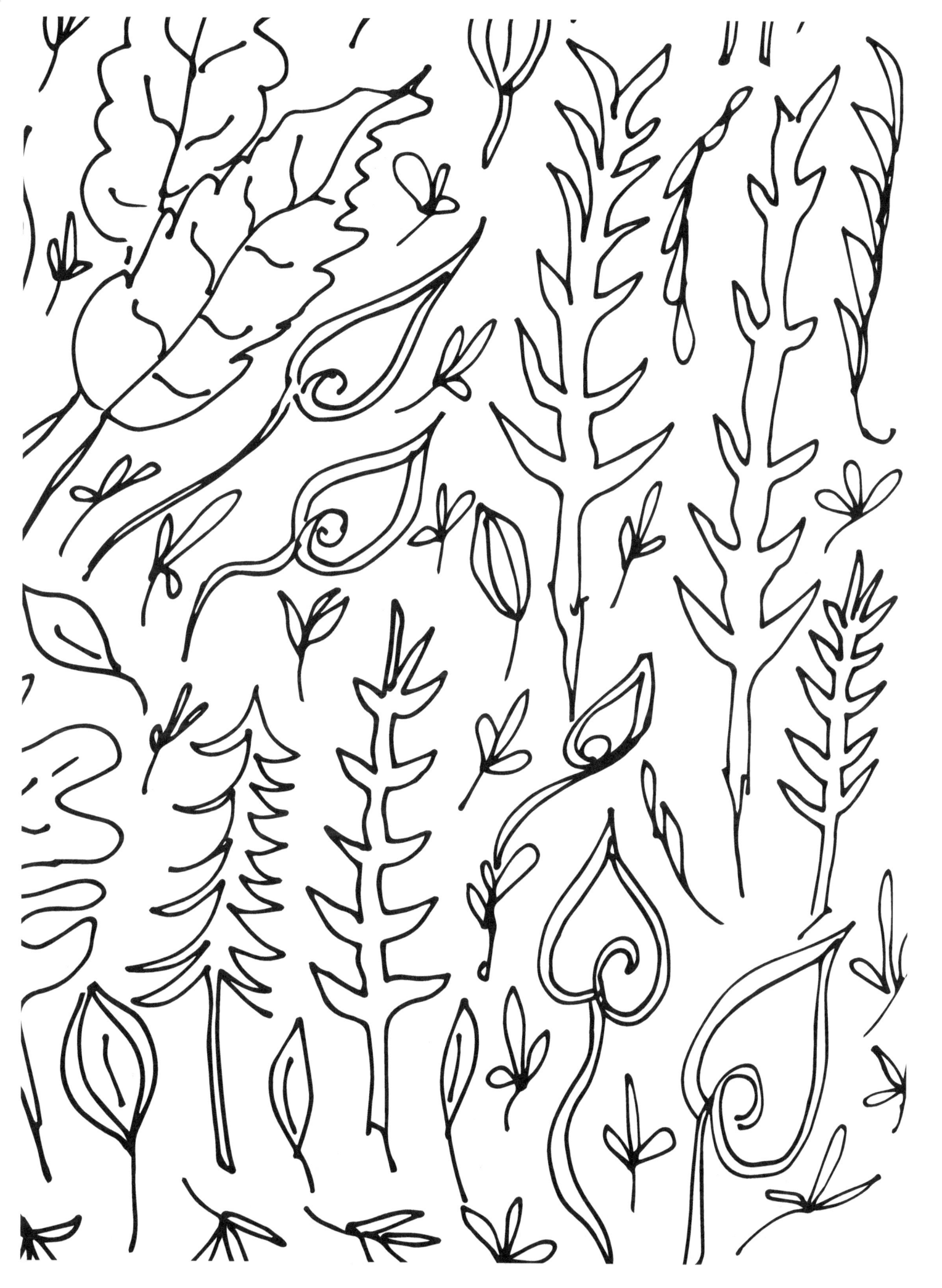

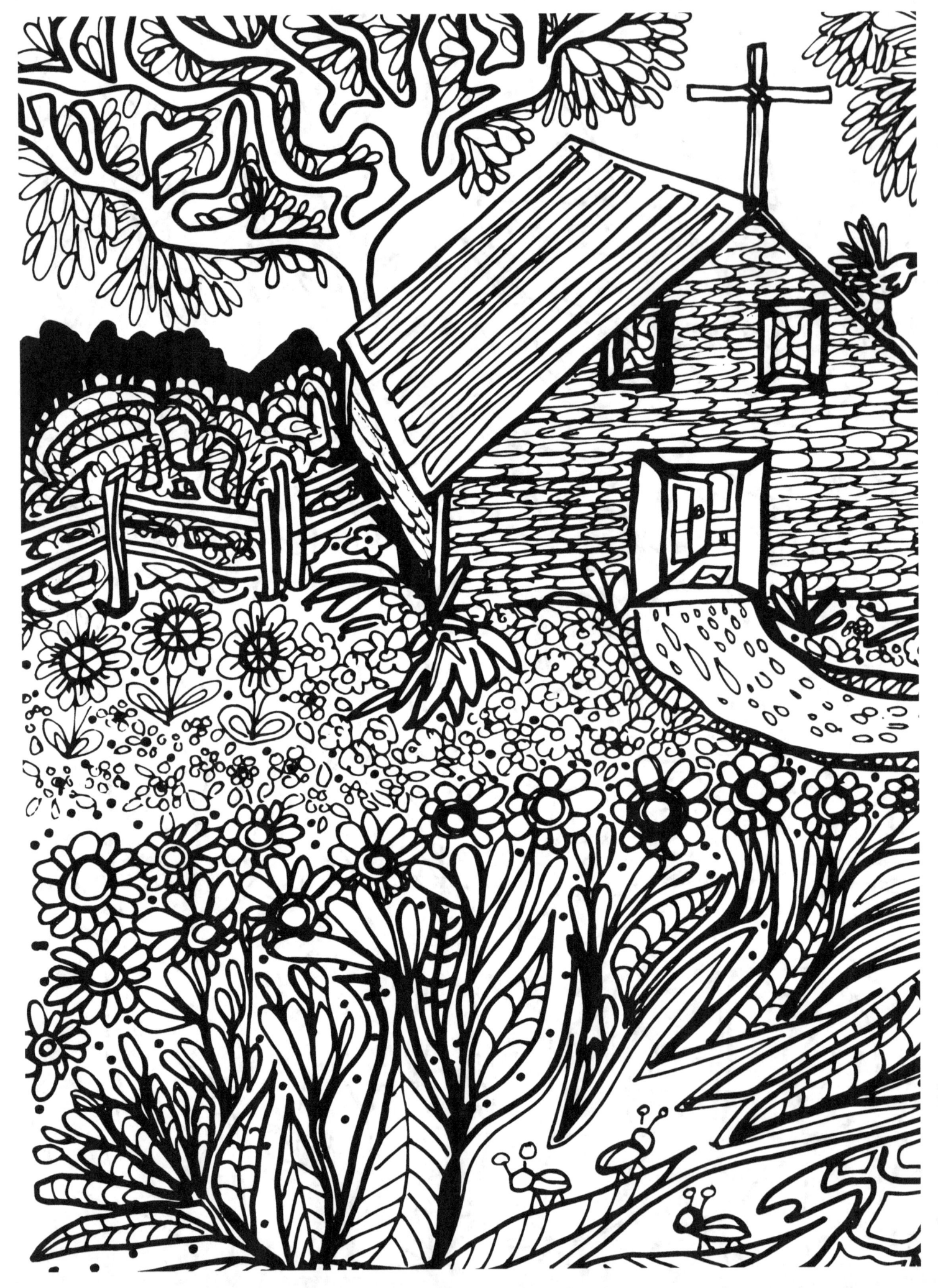

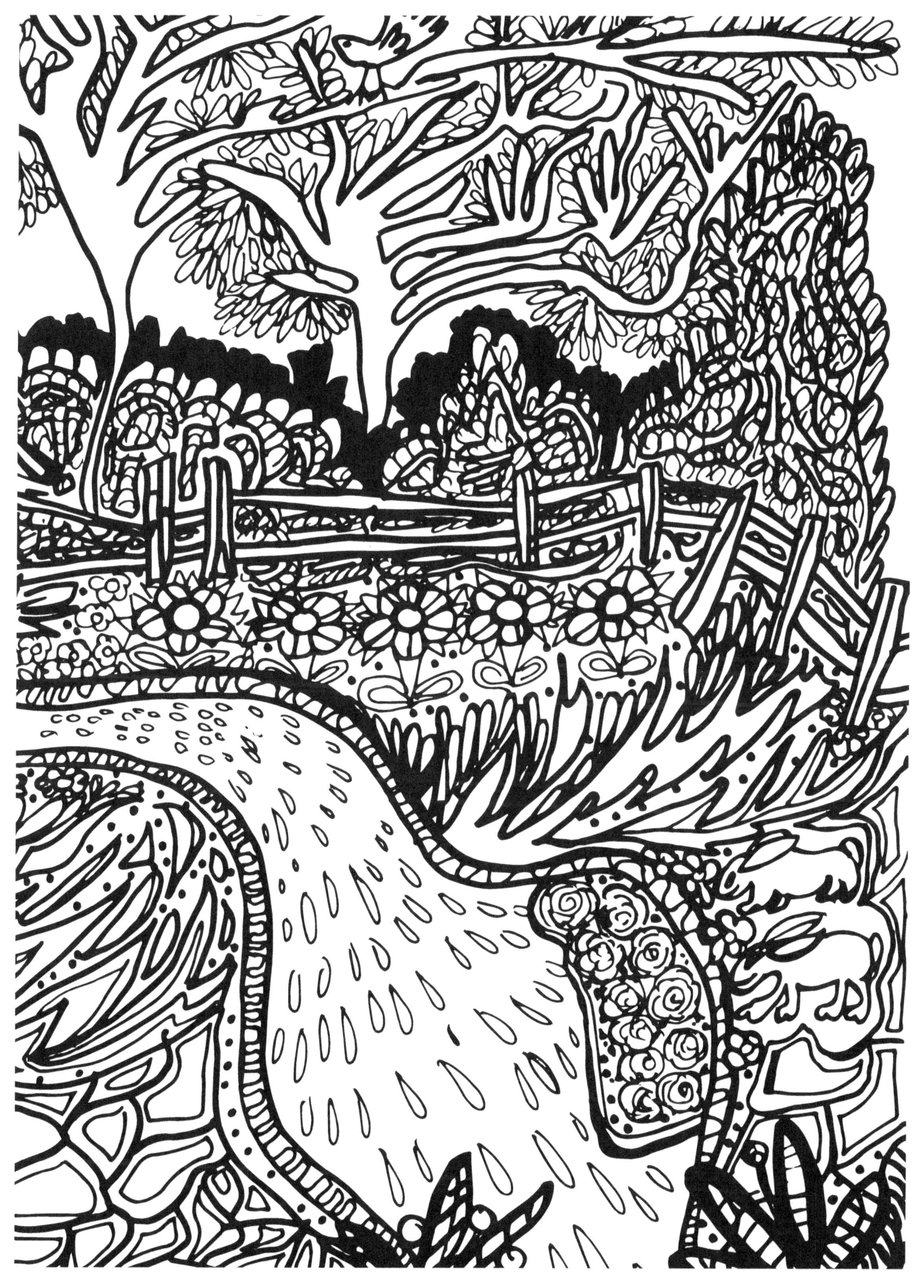

An artist cannot fail, it is a success just to be one.

Charles Cooley

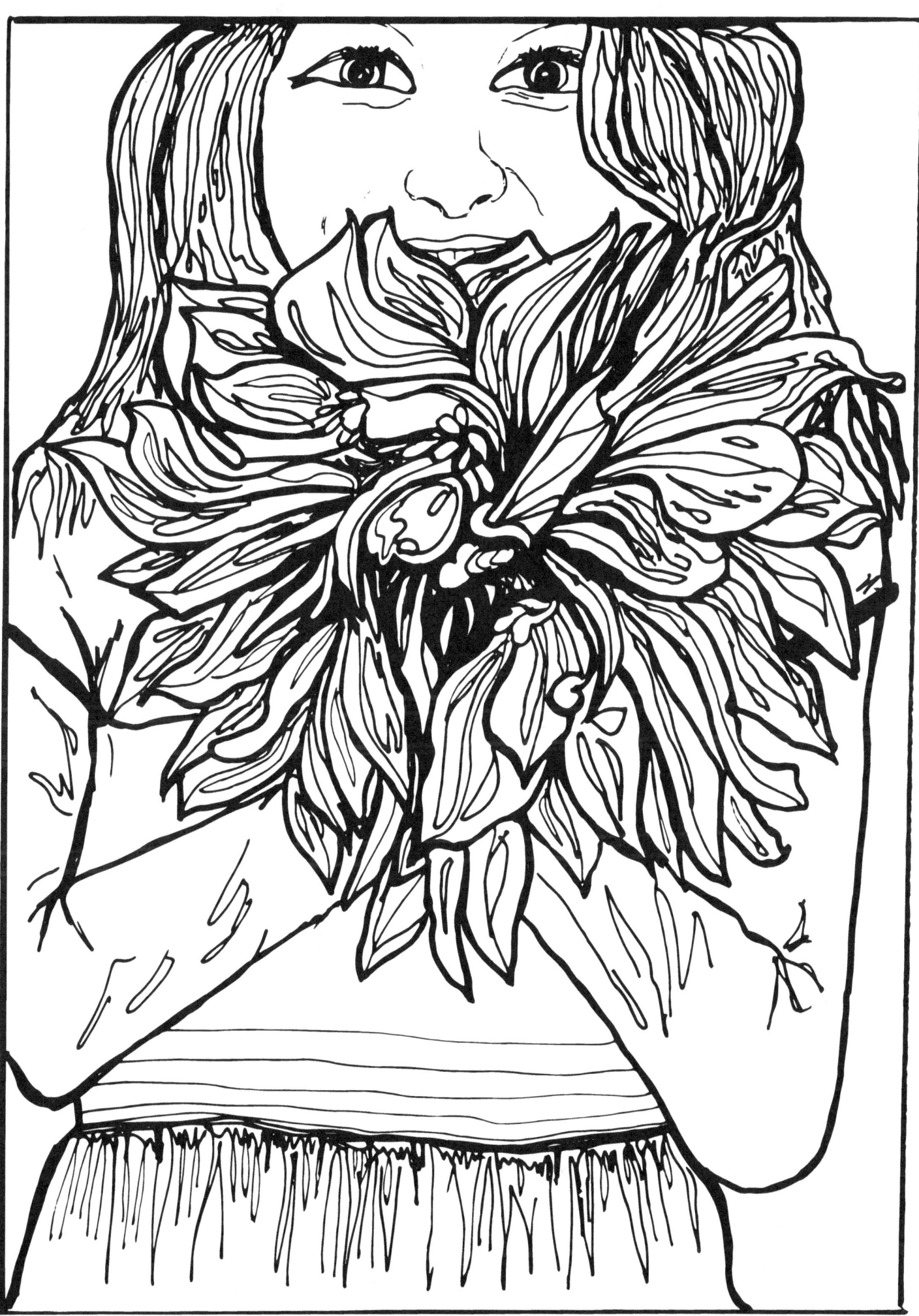

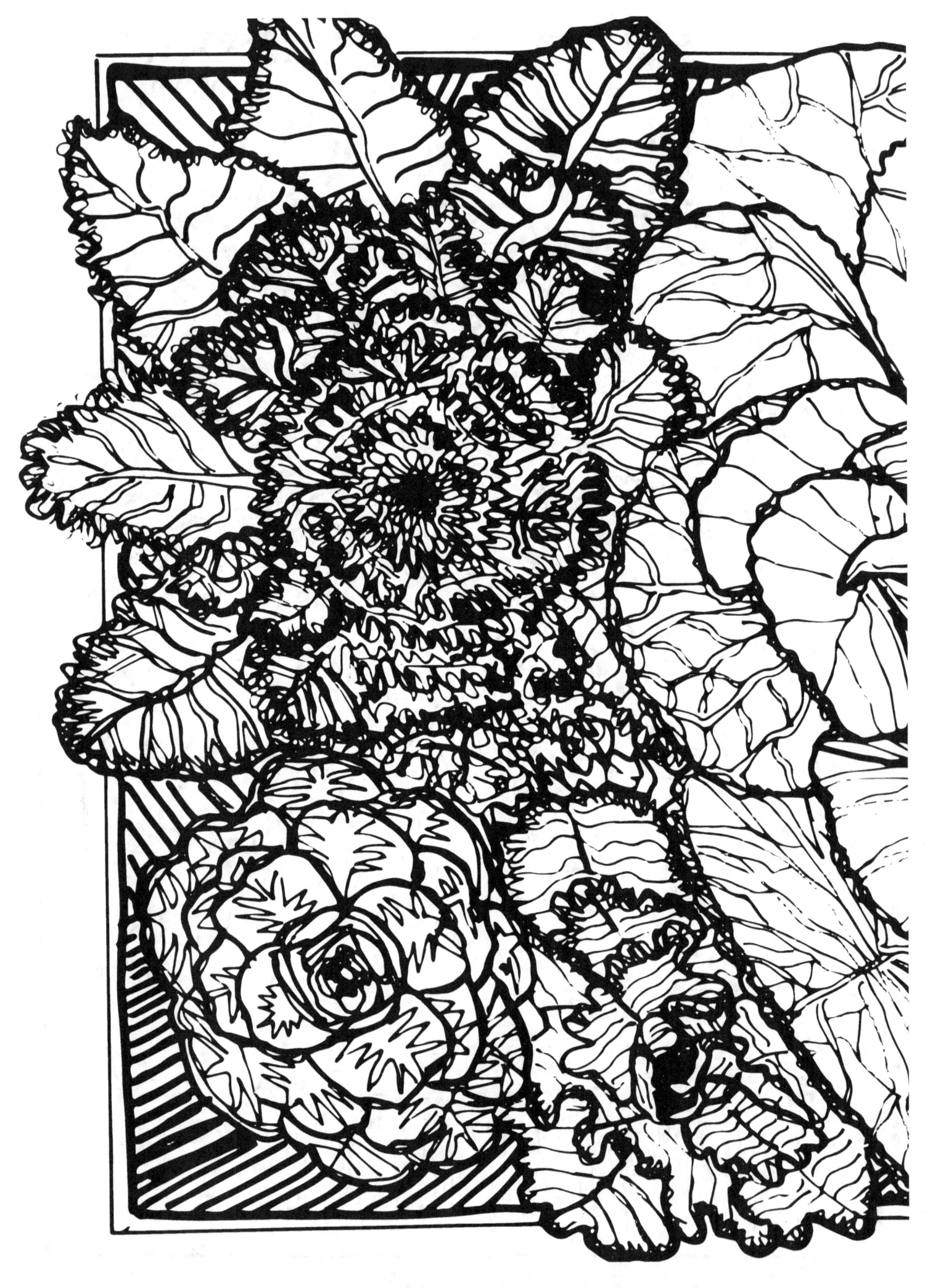

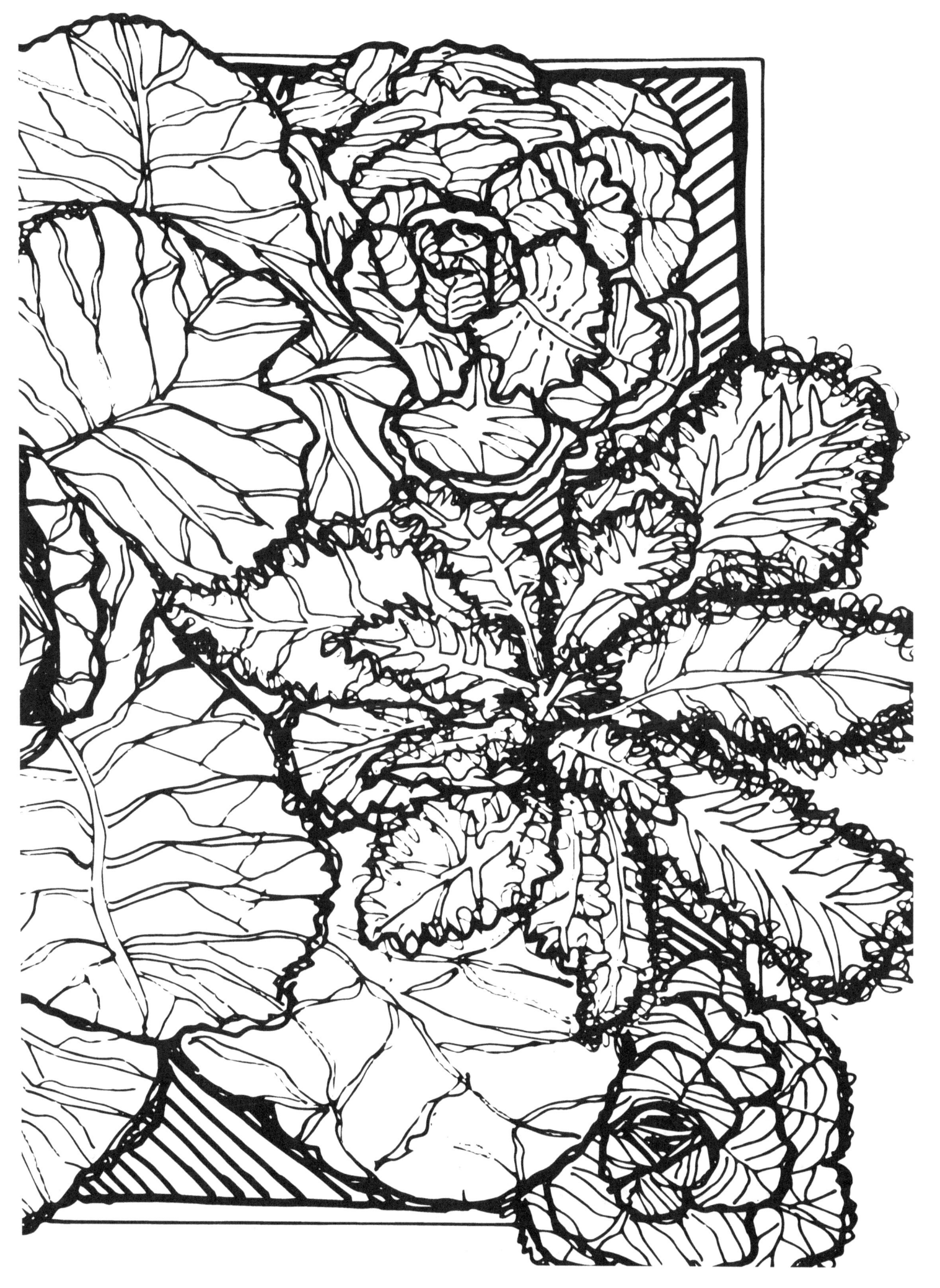

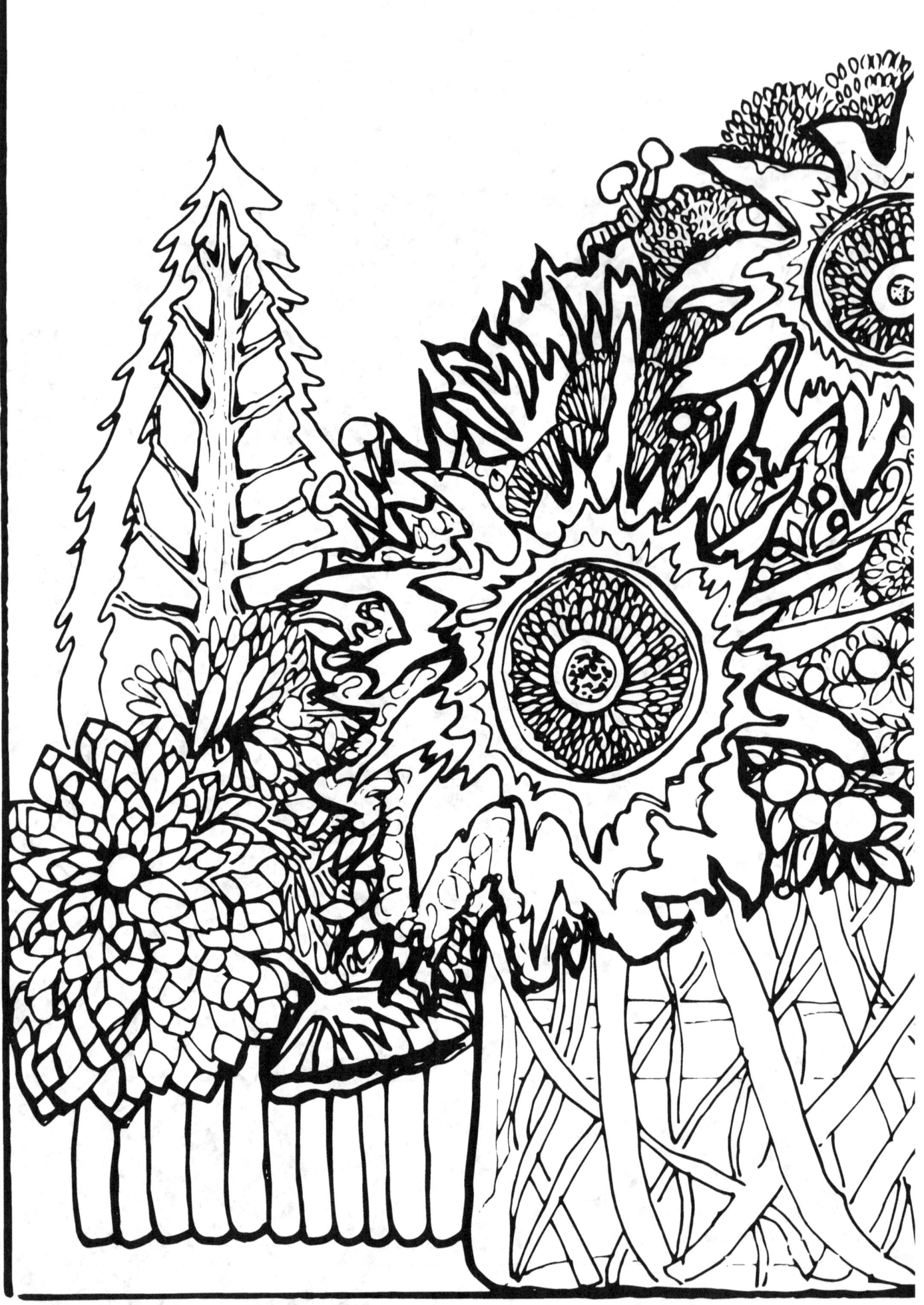

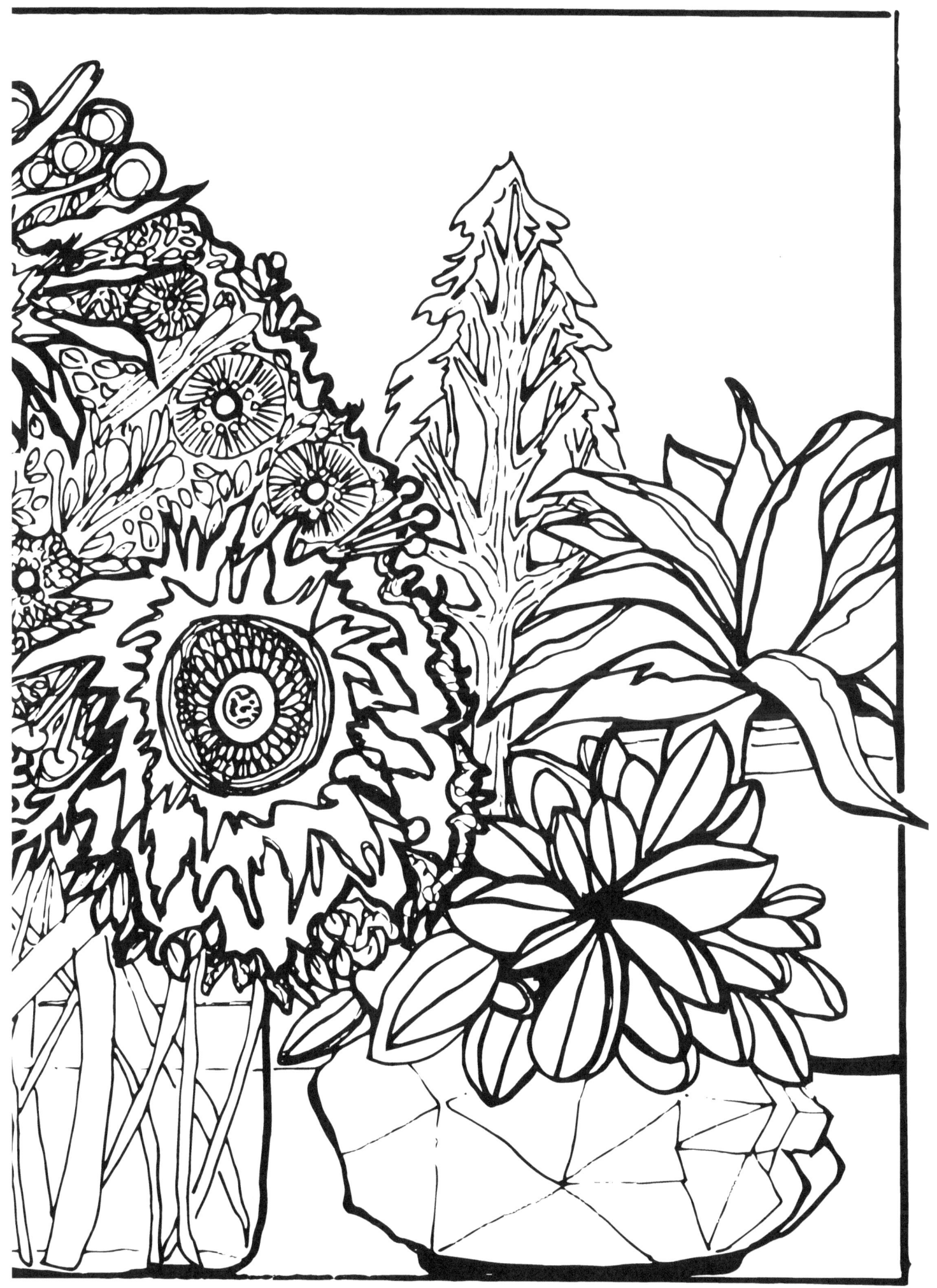

You can't use up creativity. The more you use the more you have.

Maya Angelou

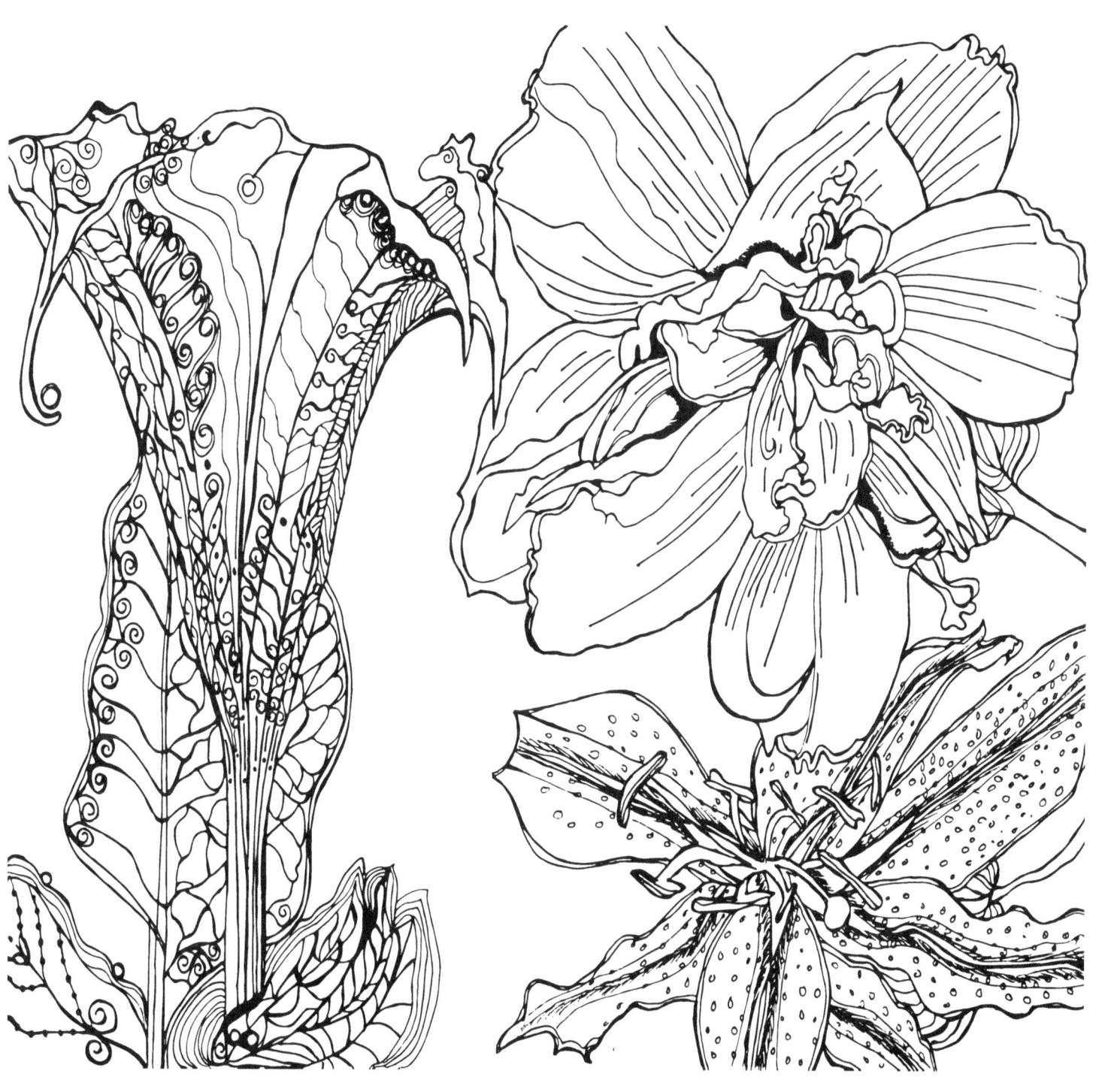

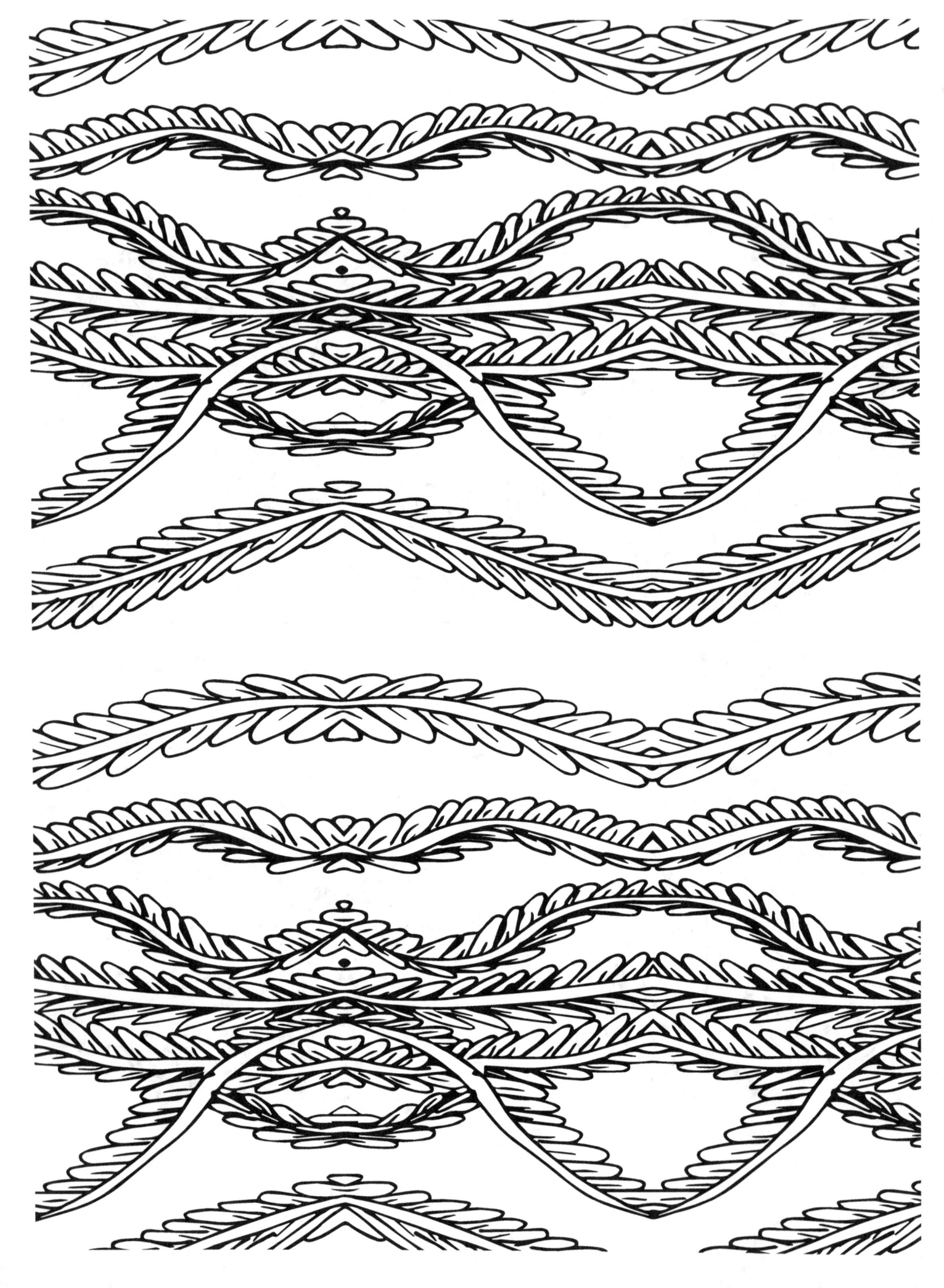

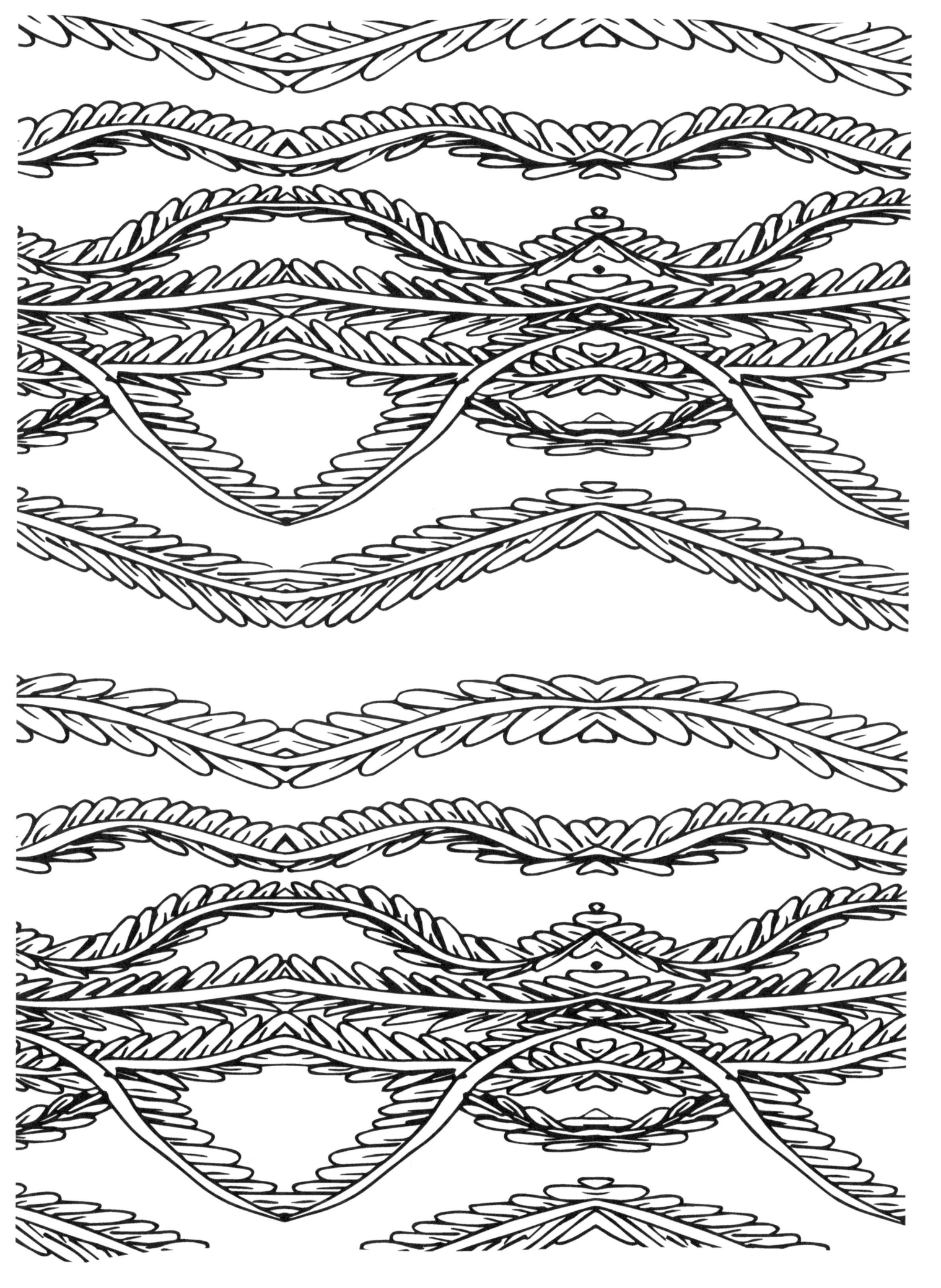

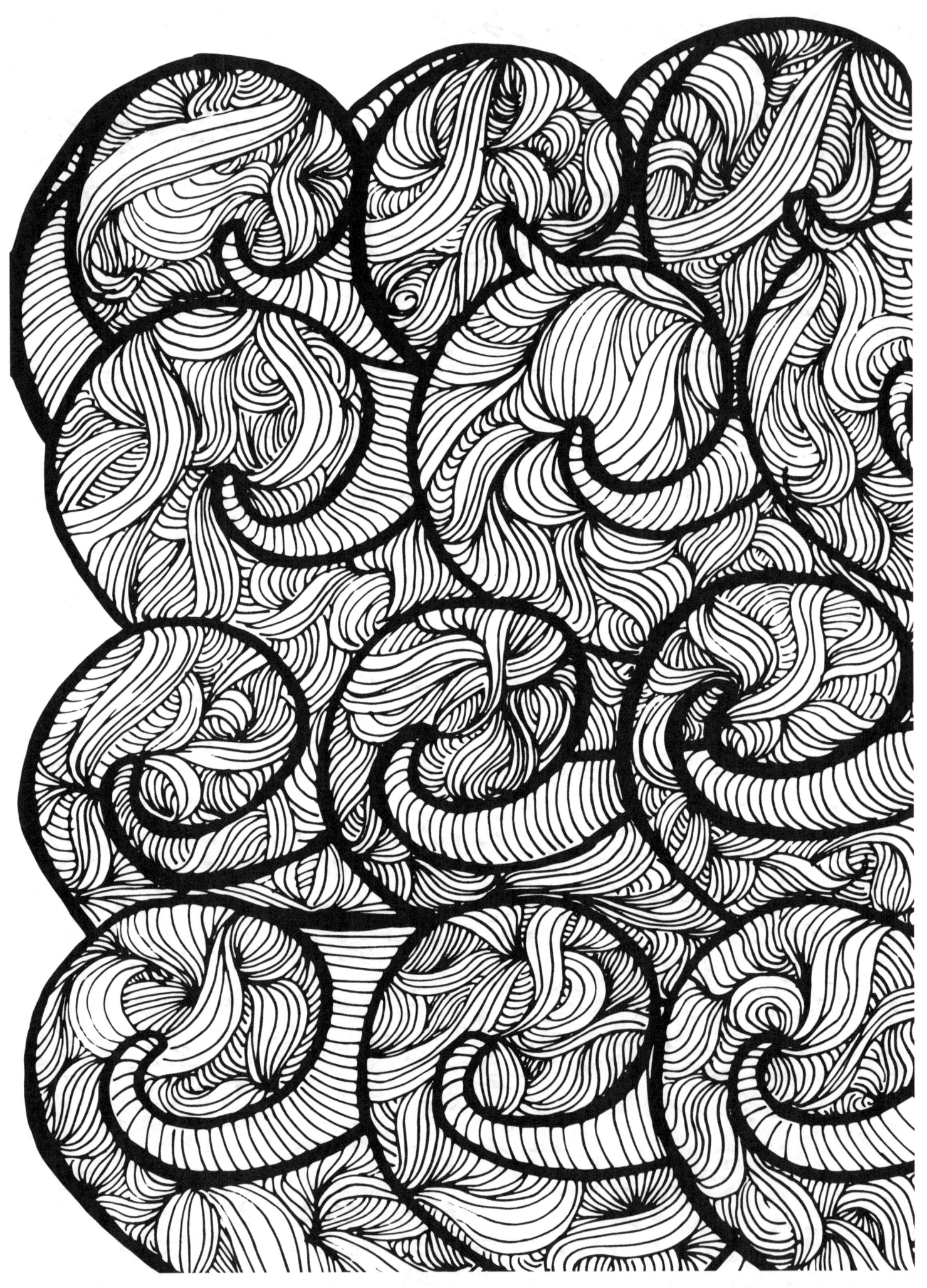

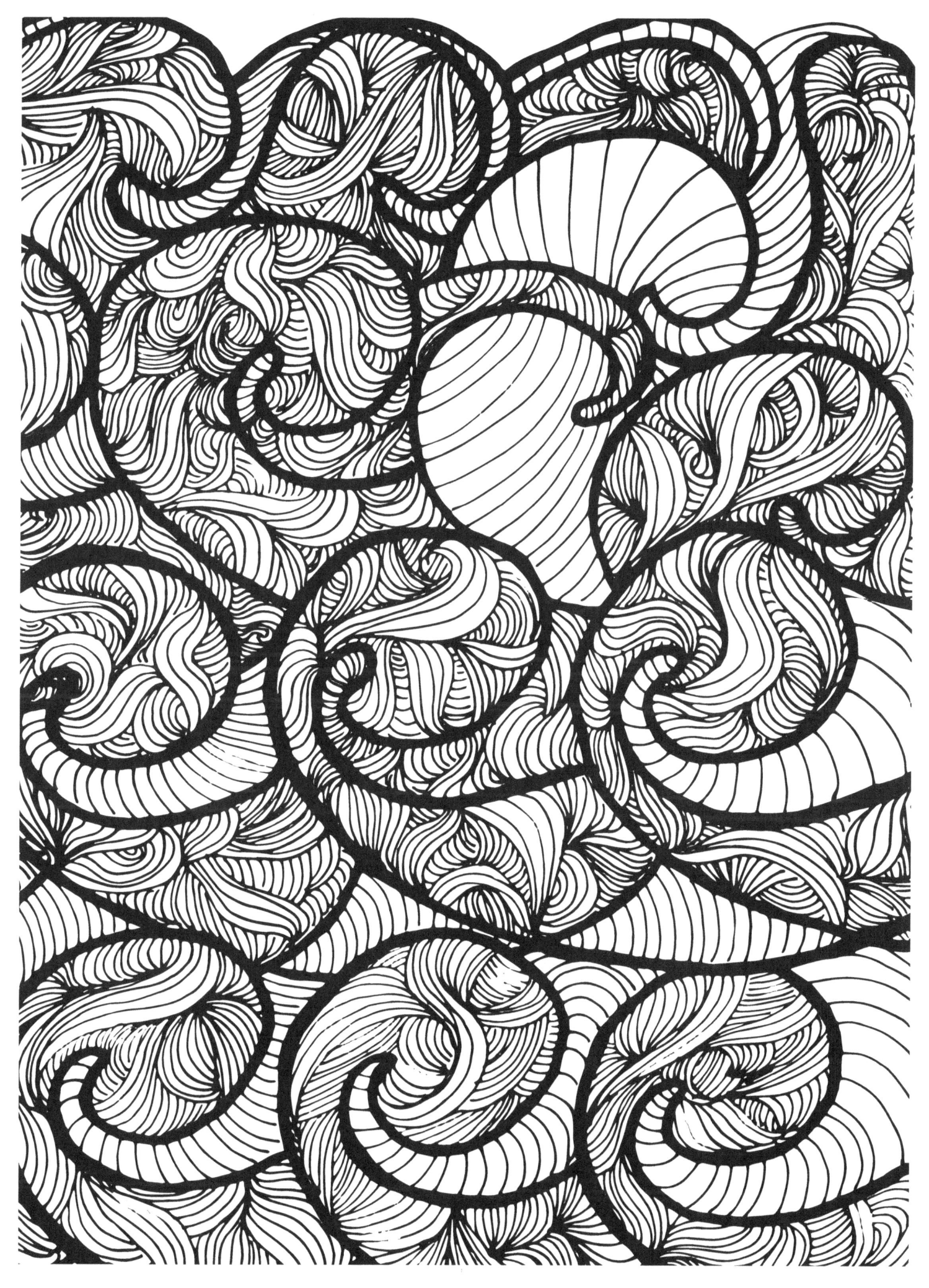

Where the spirit does not work with the hand there is no art.

Leonardo Da Vinci

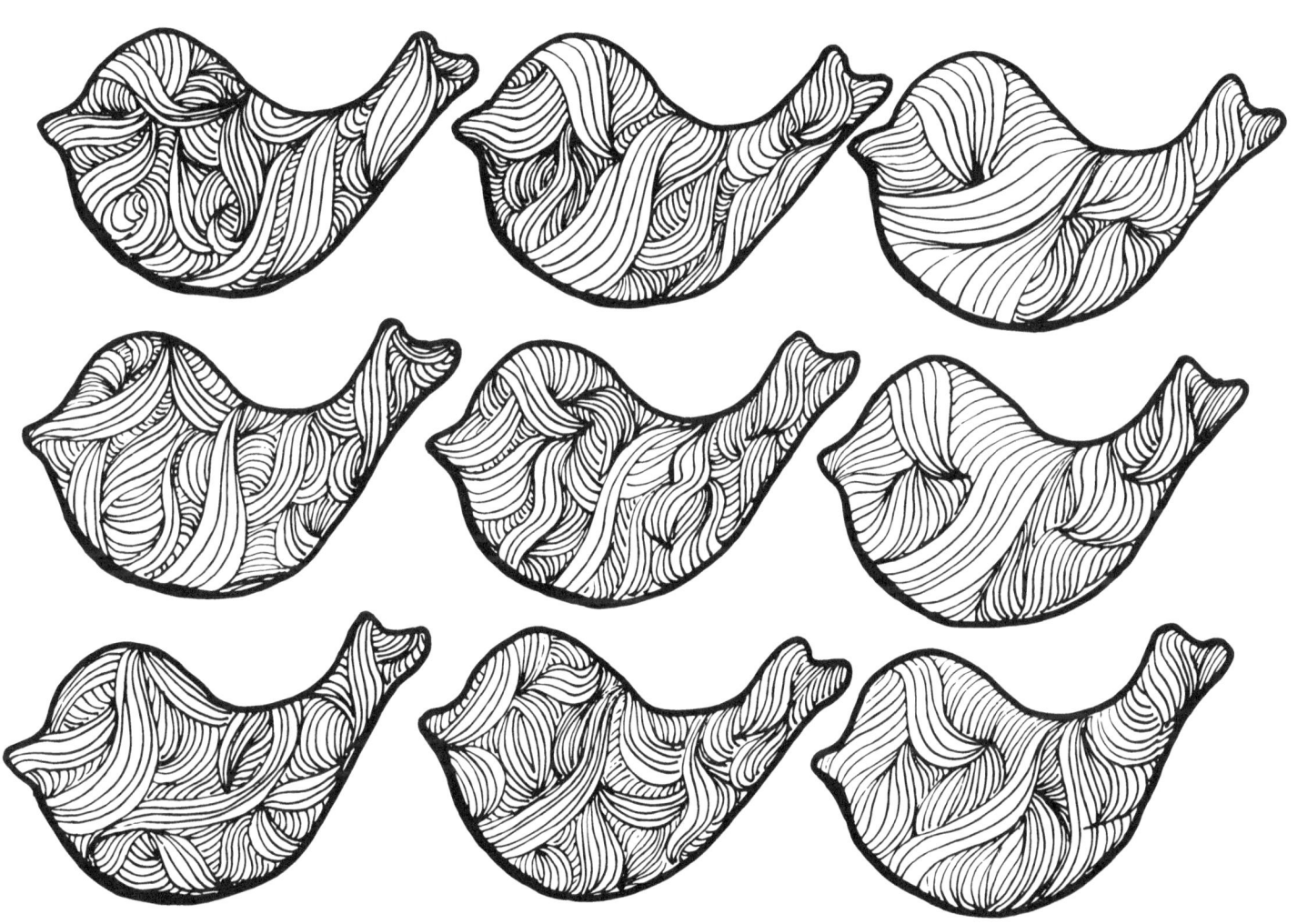

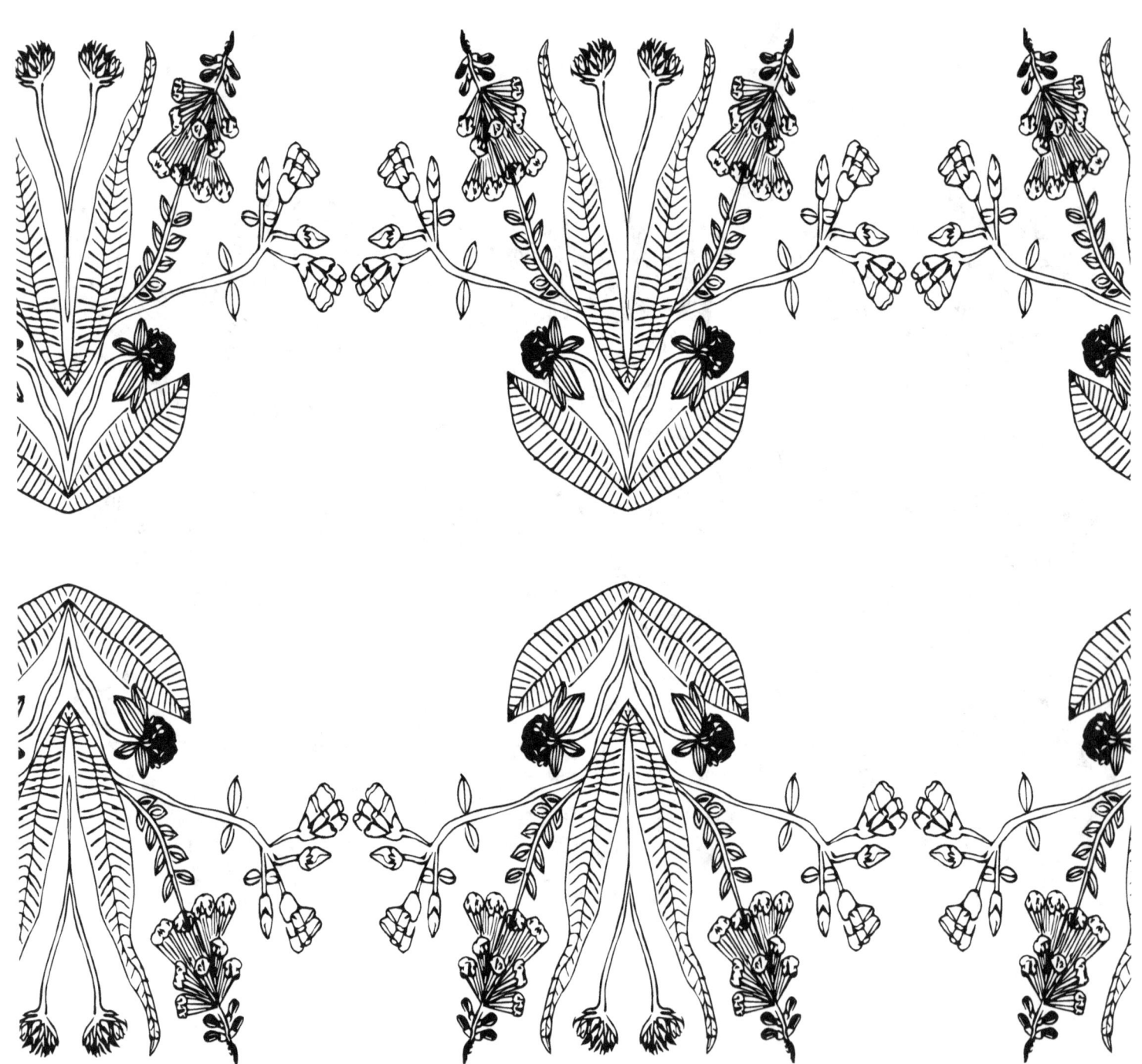

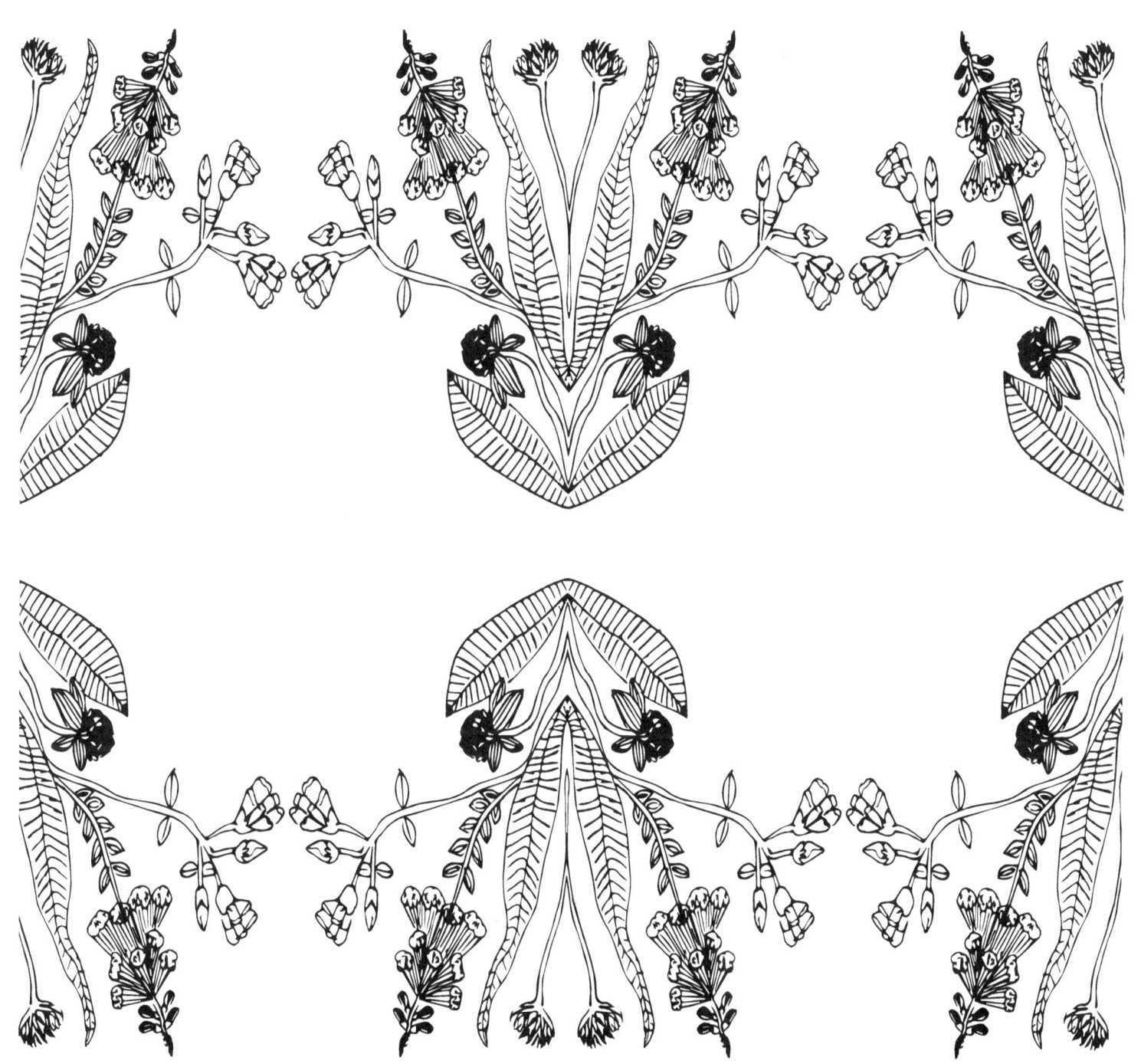

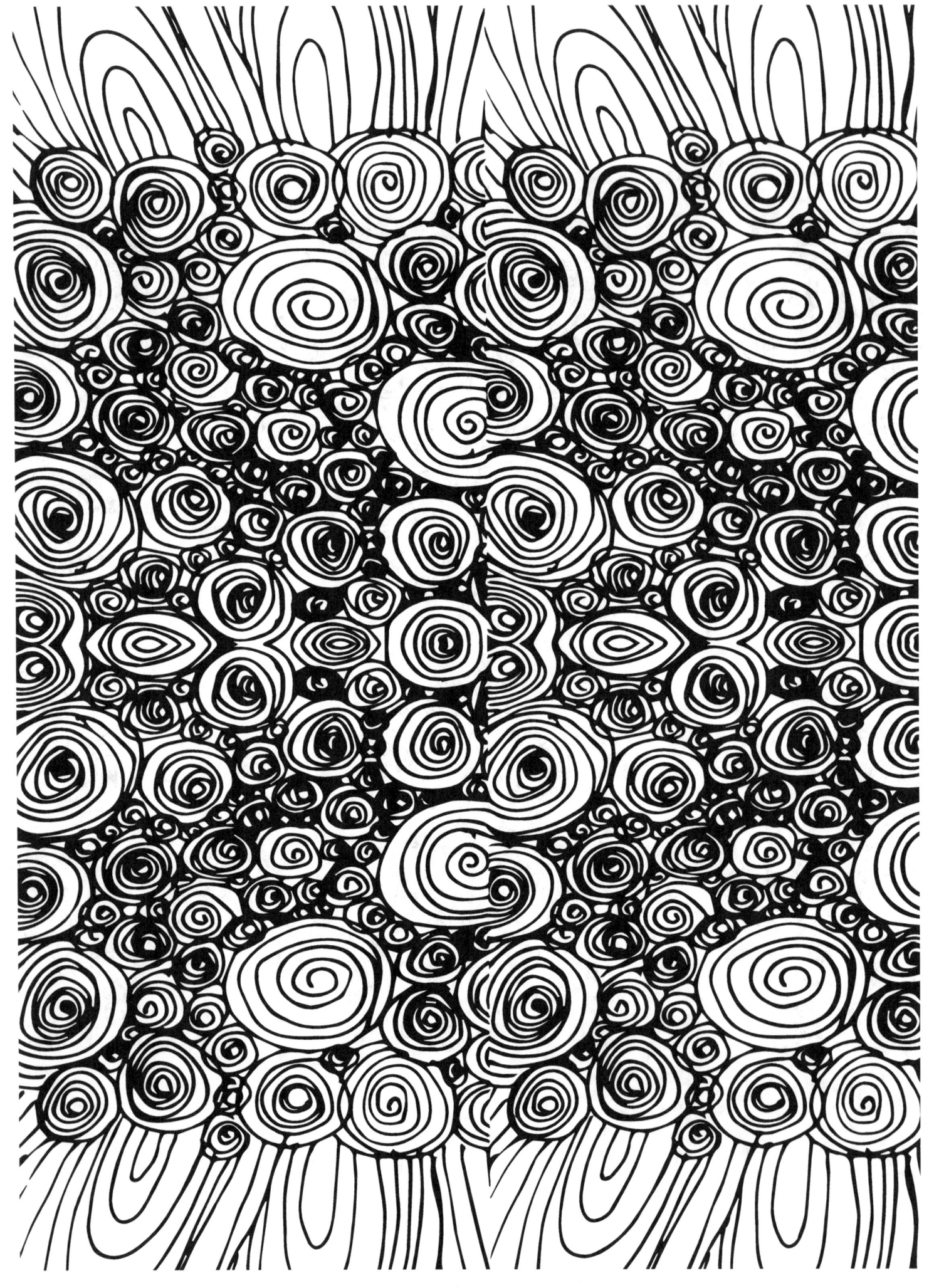

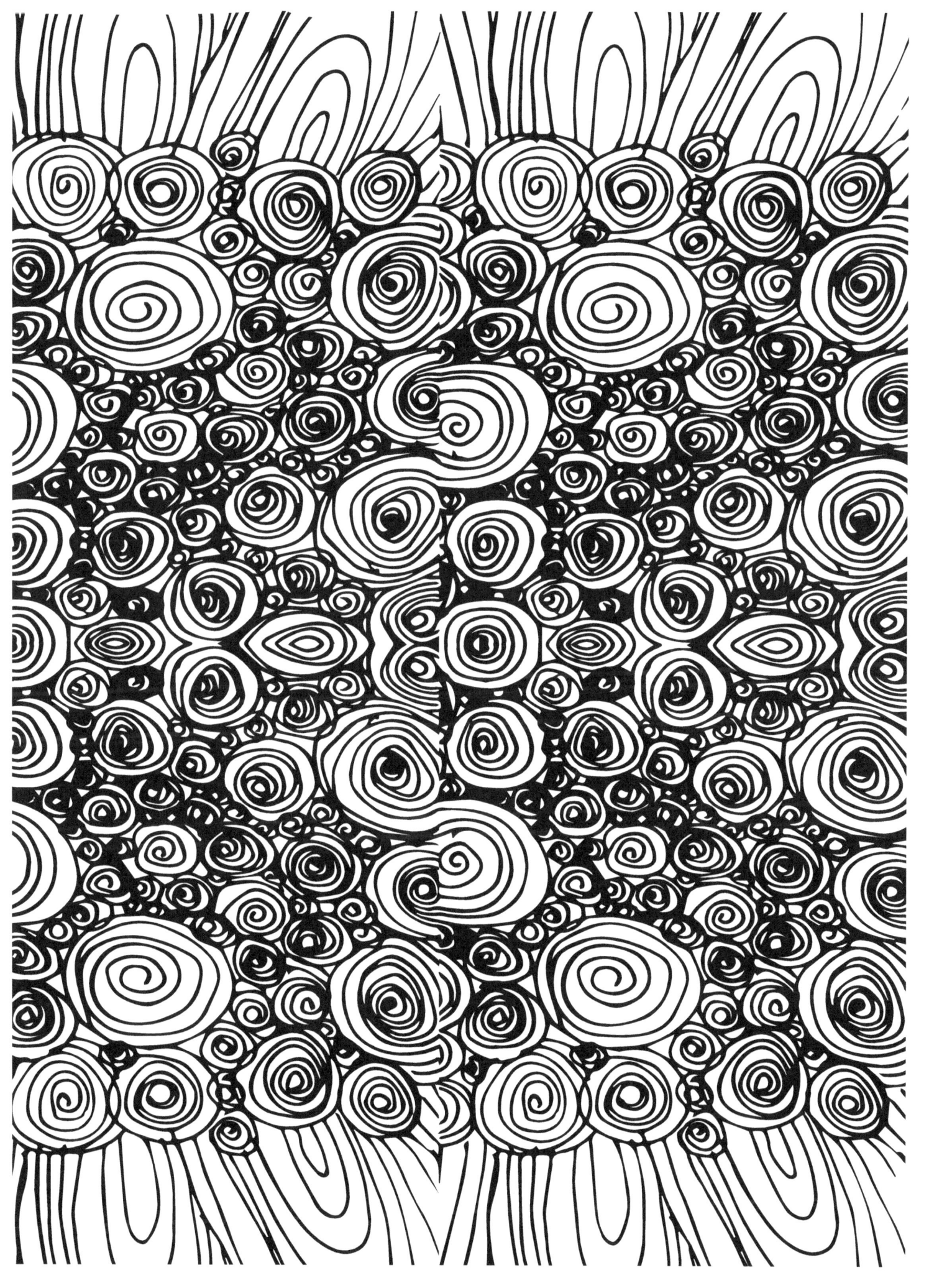

Creativity is everywhere and is for everyone. You don't need to be a genius, you just need to be yourself.

Austin Kleon

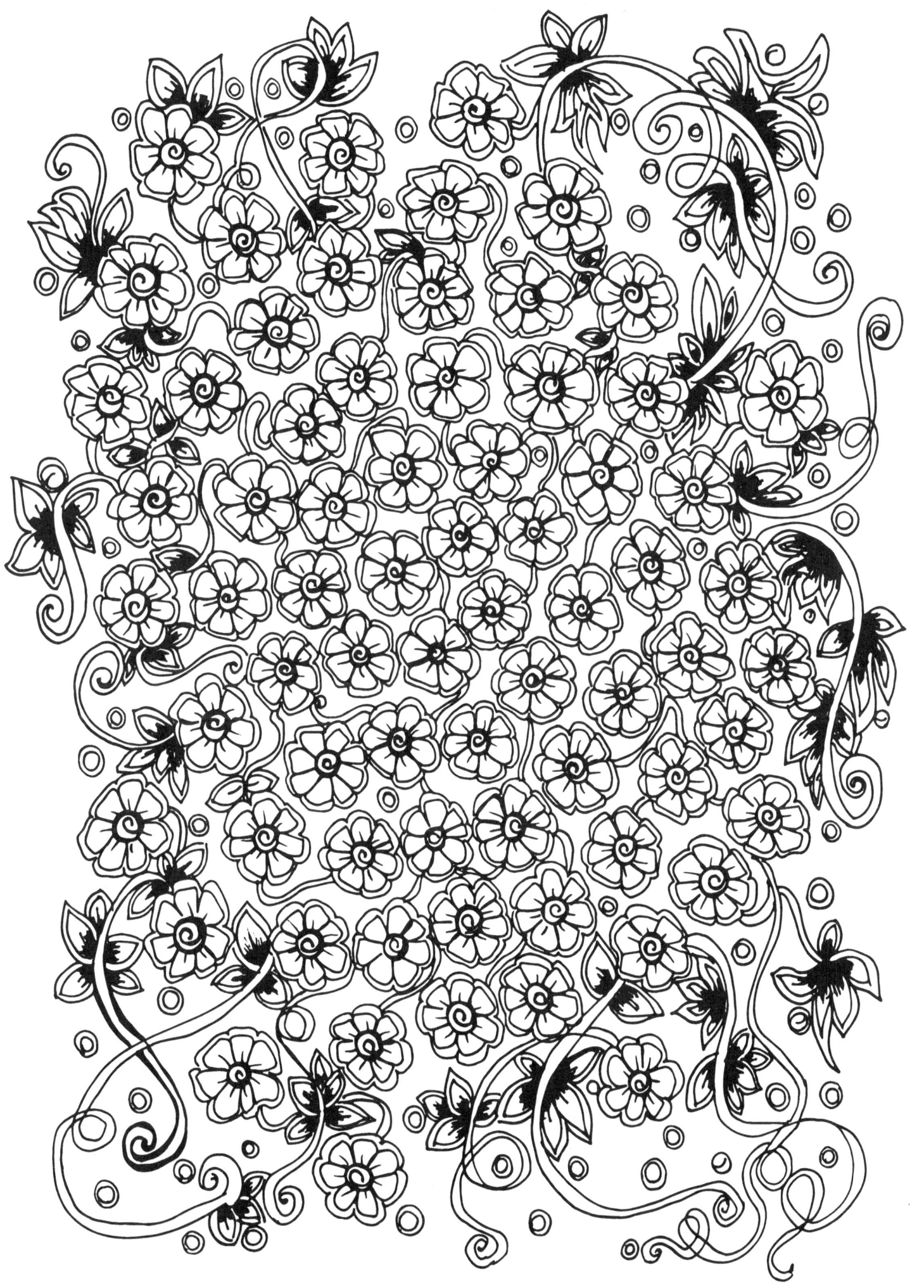

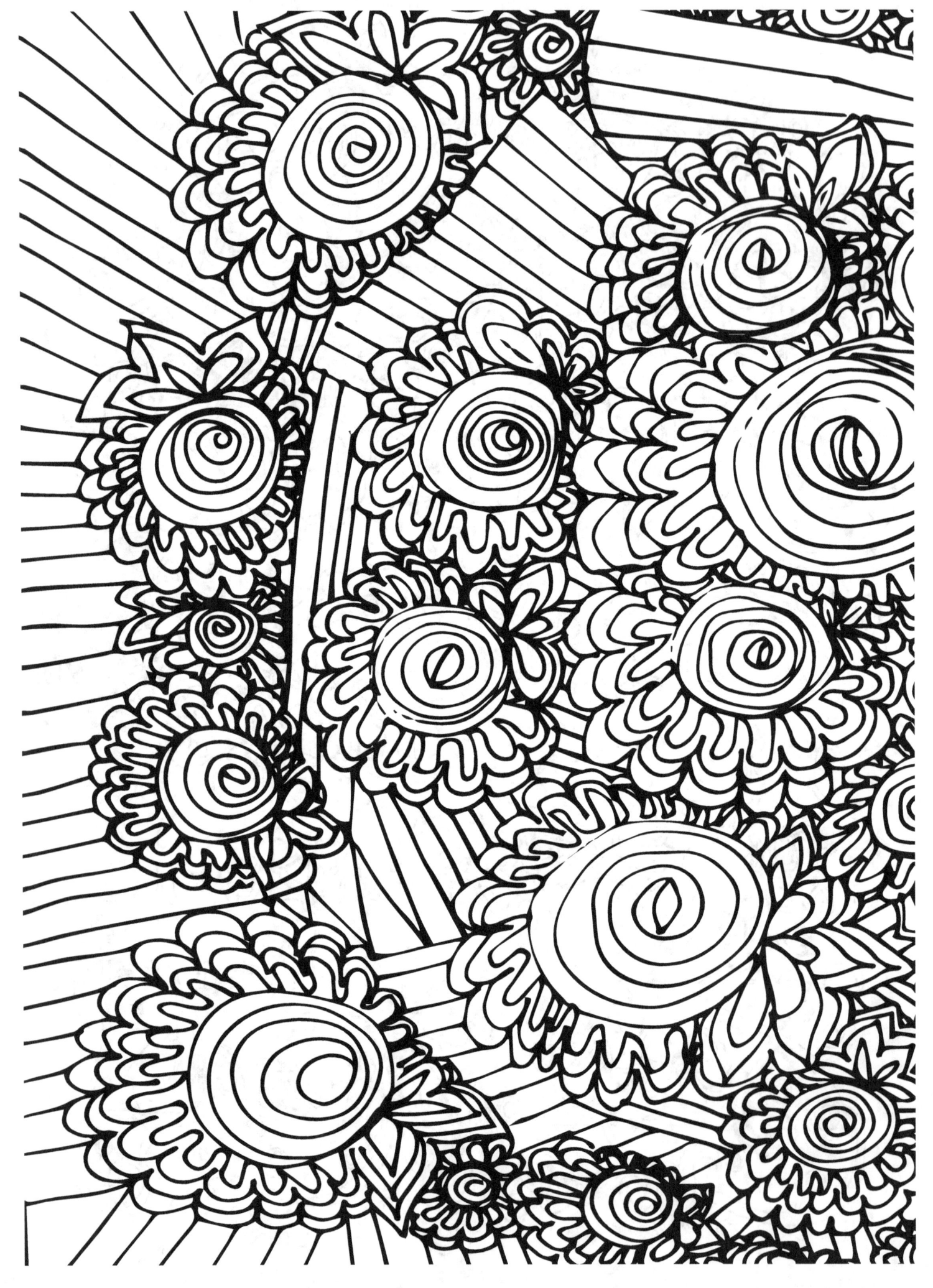

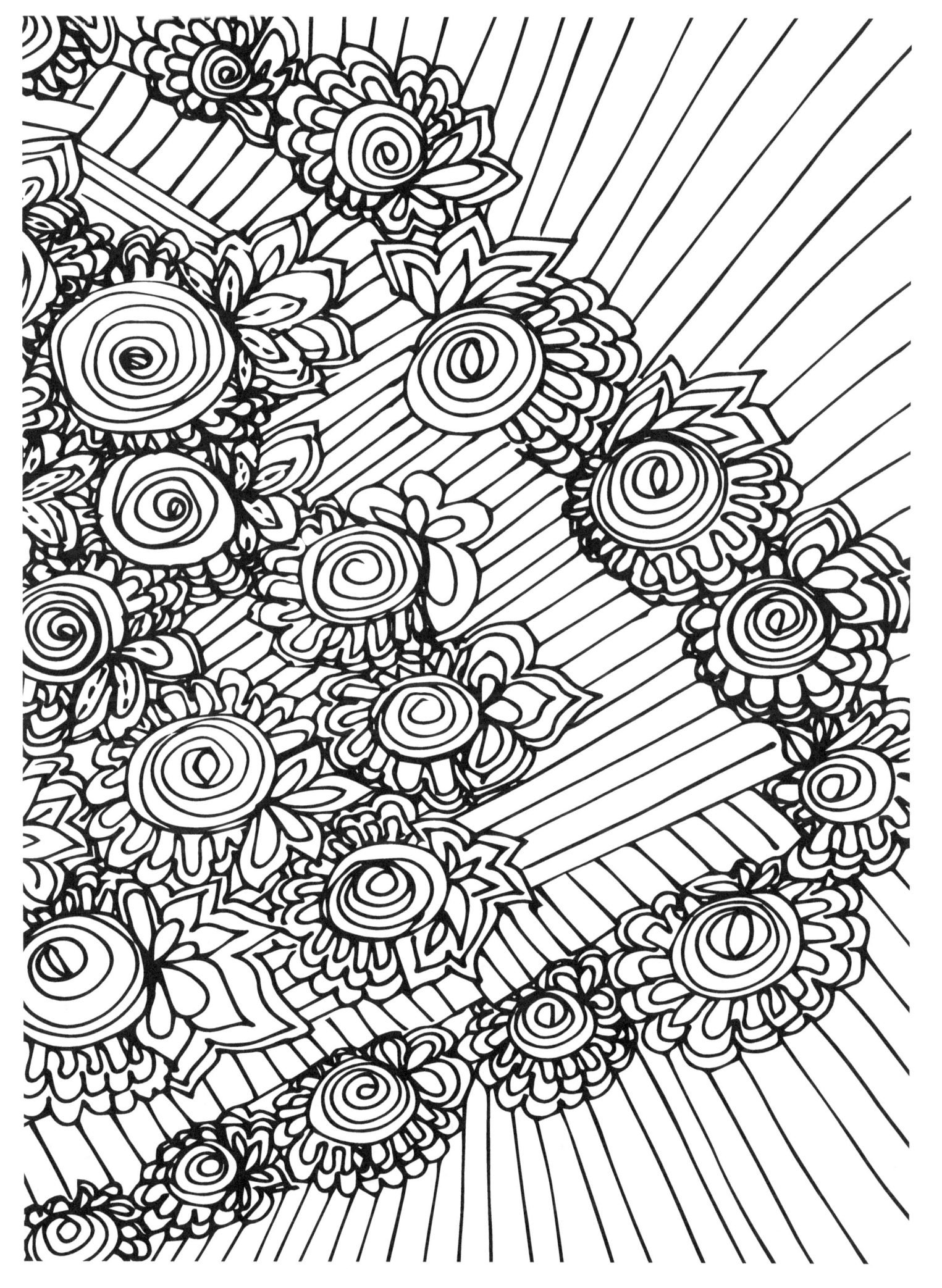

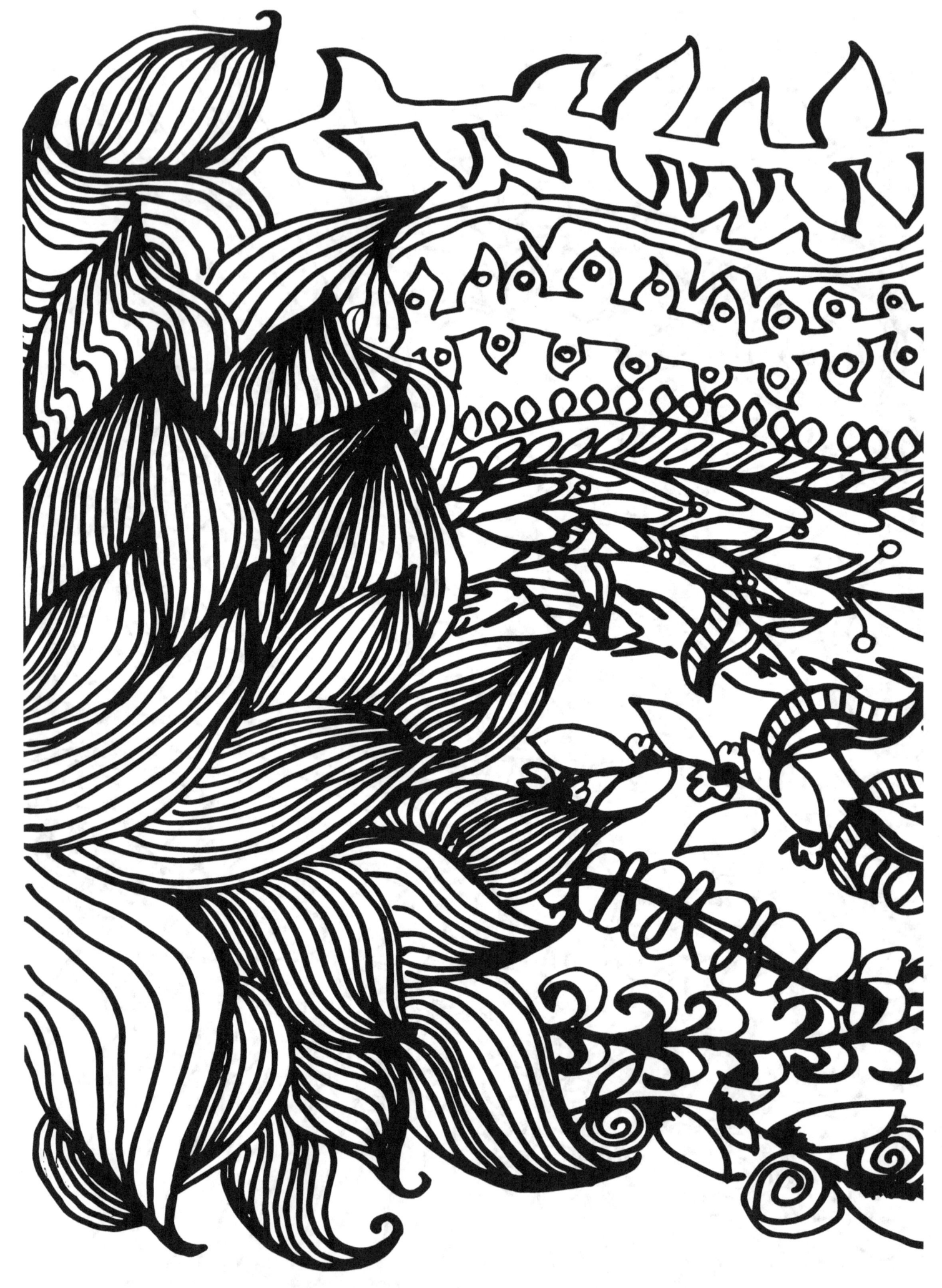

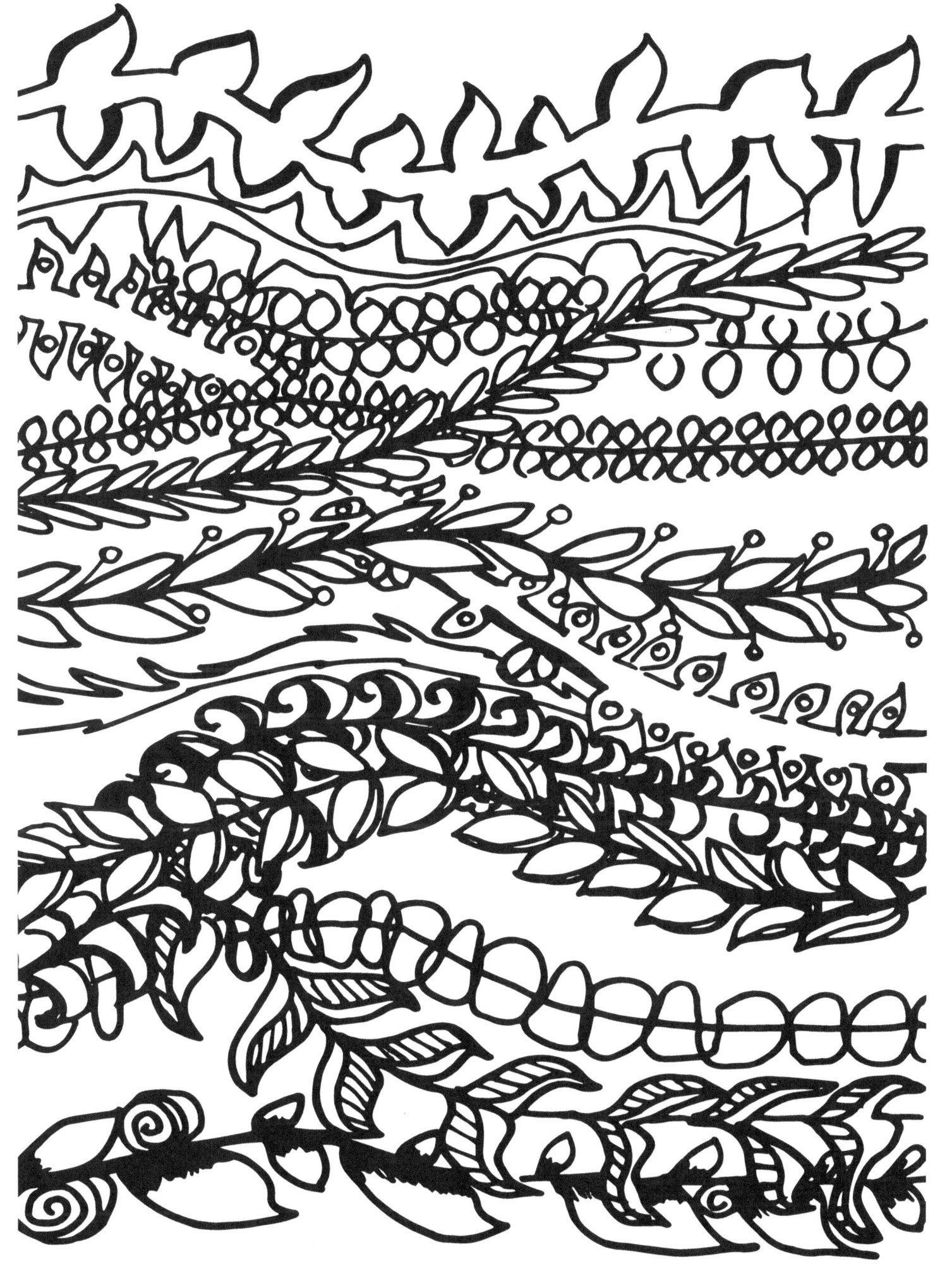

Art is important. We tend to think it is a luxury, but it gives people deep pleasure because beauty is the personification of hope that something grander is at work.

Gil Dellinger

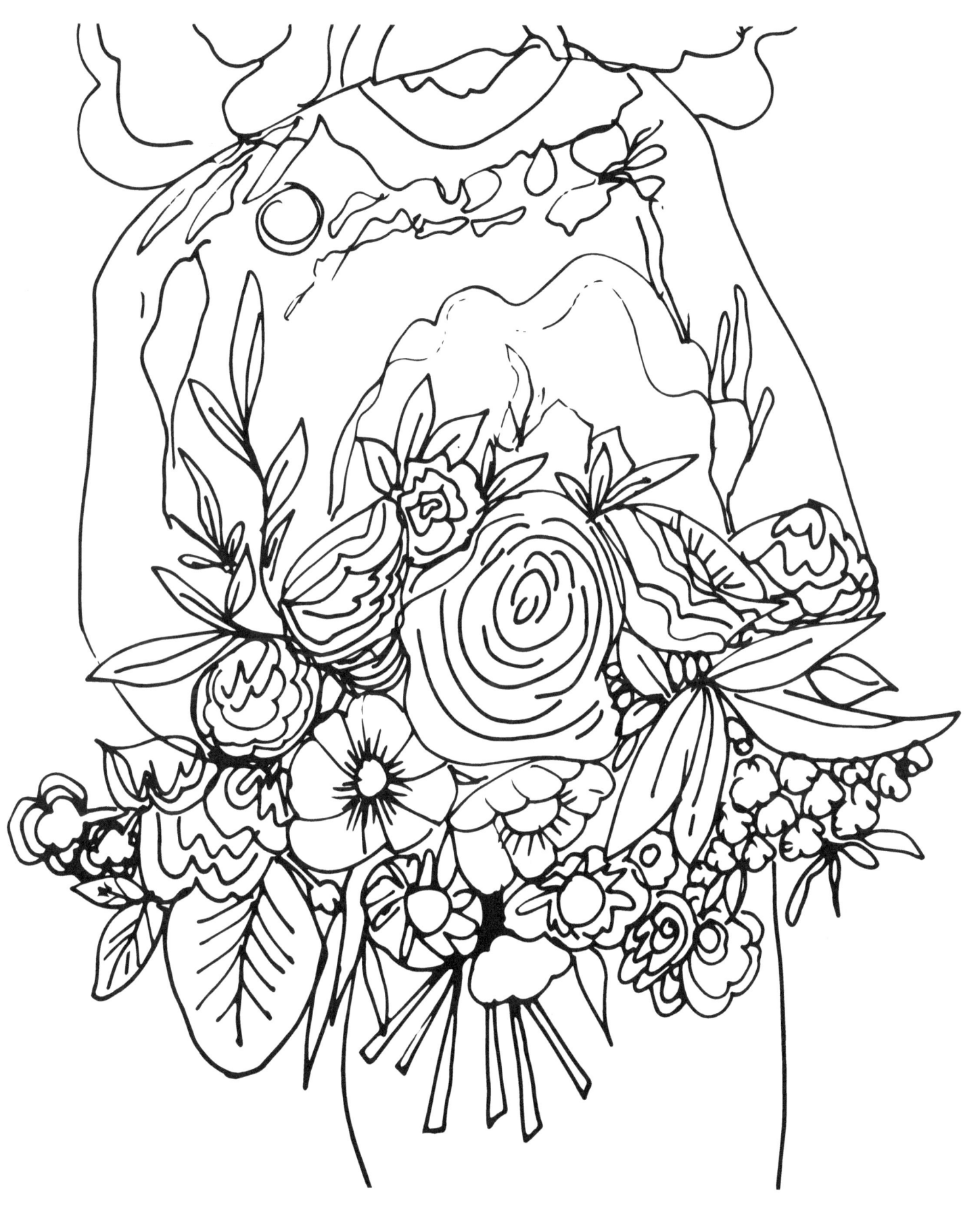

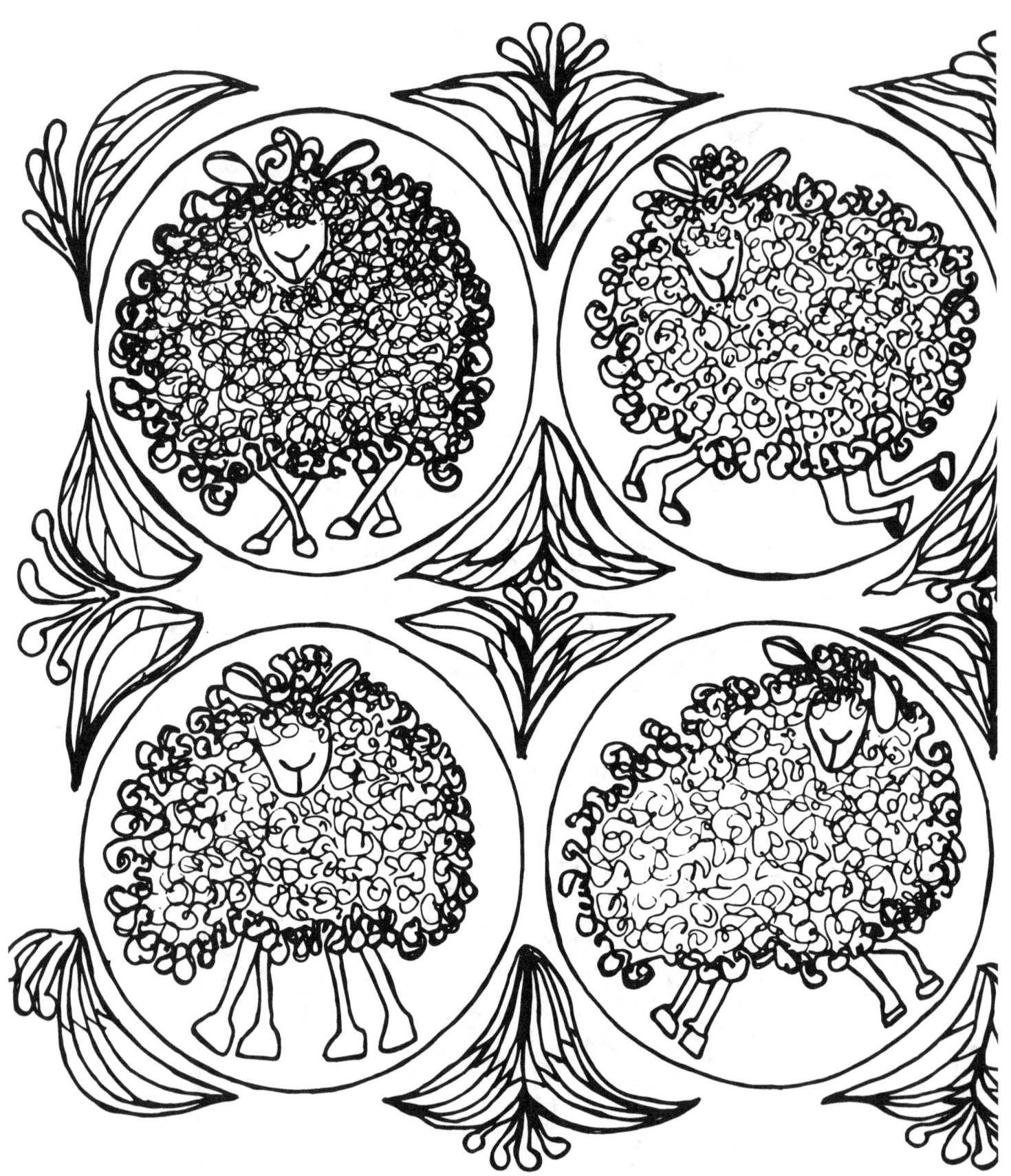

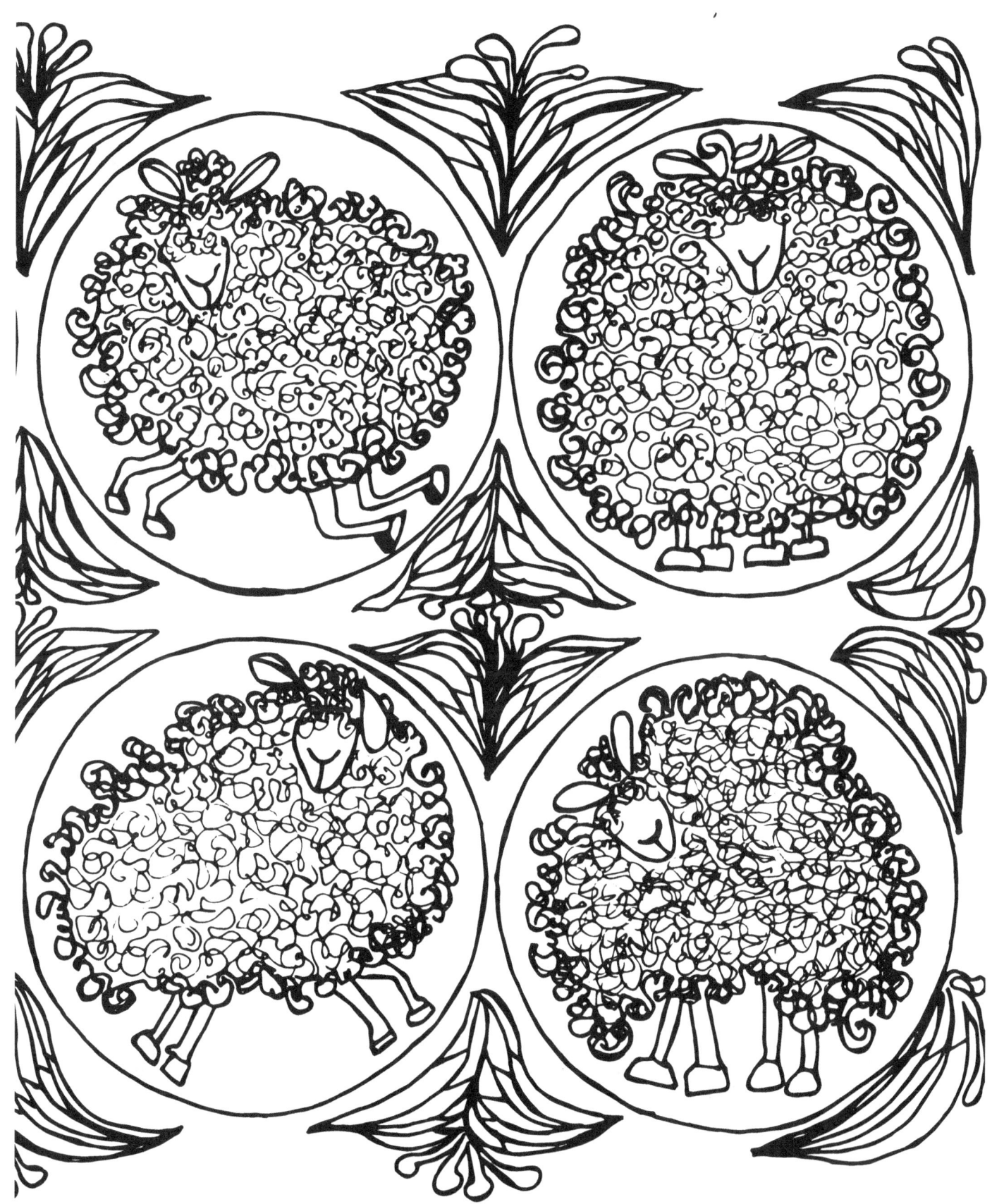

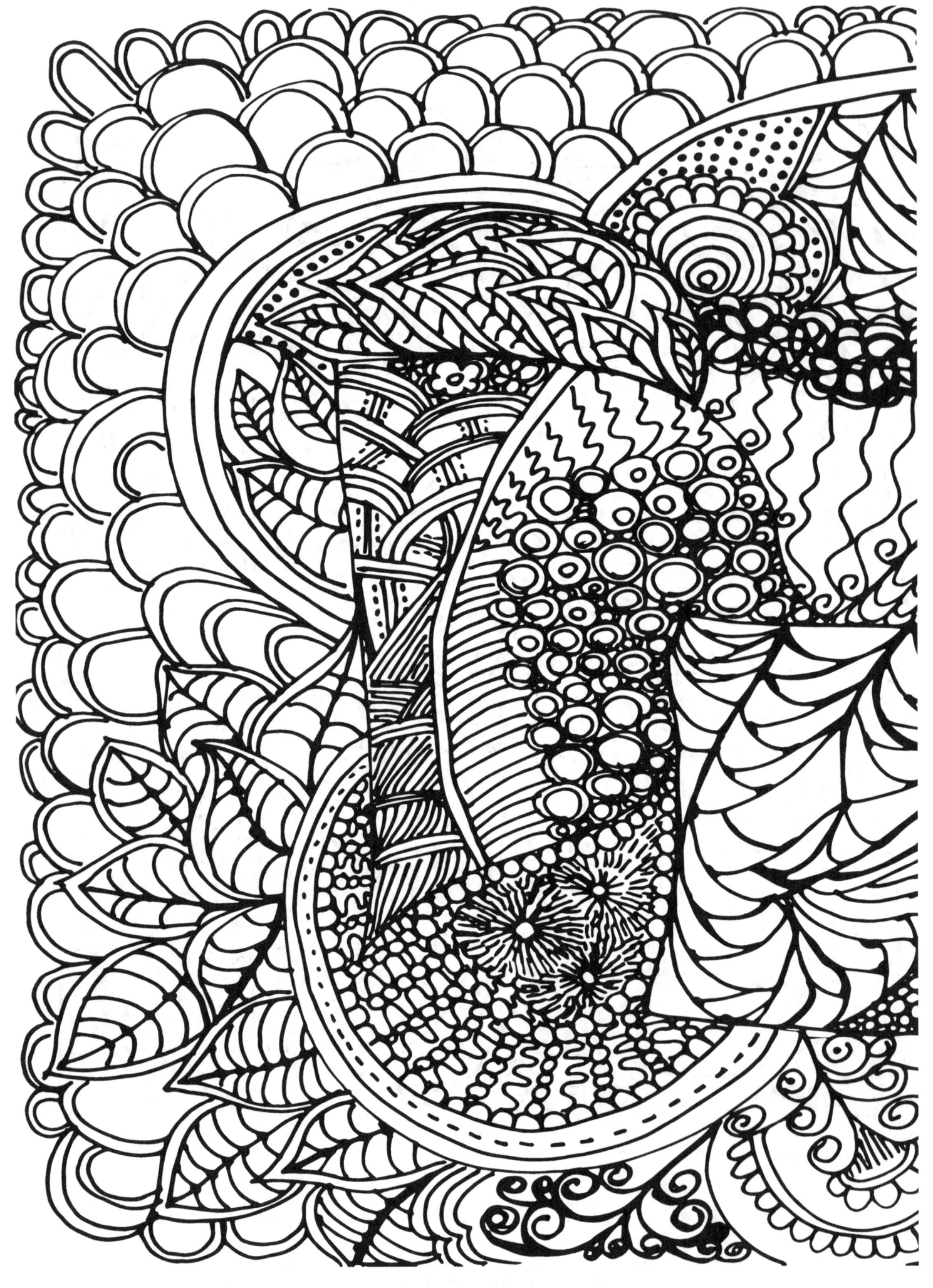

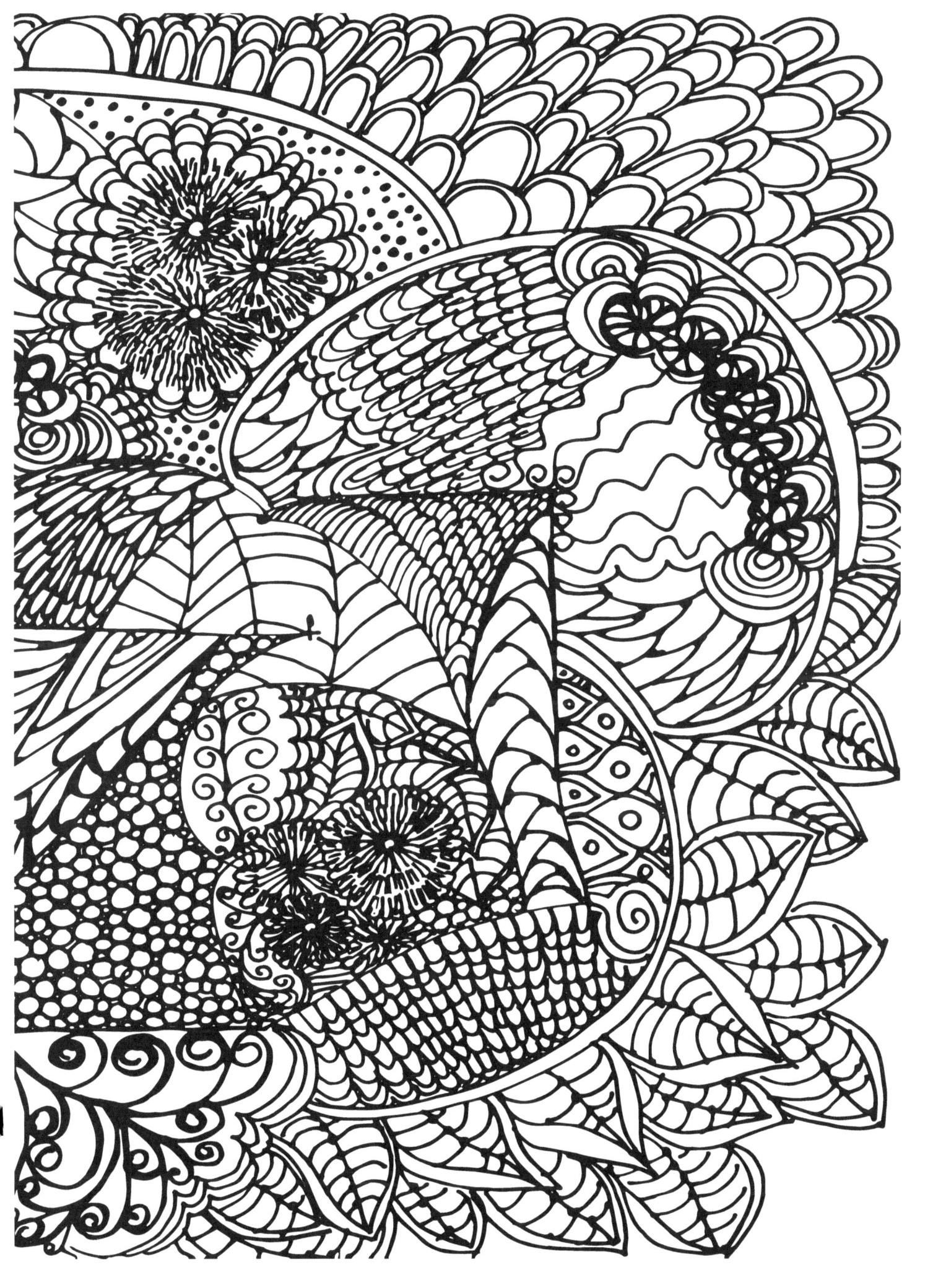

**Work of sight is done. Now do heart work
on the pictures within you.**

Rainer Maria Rilke

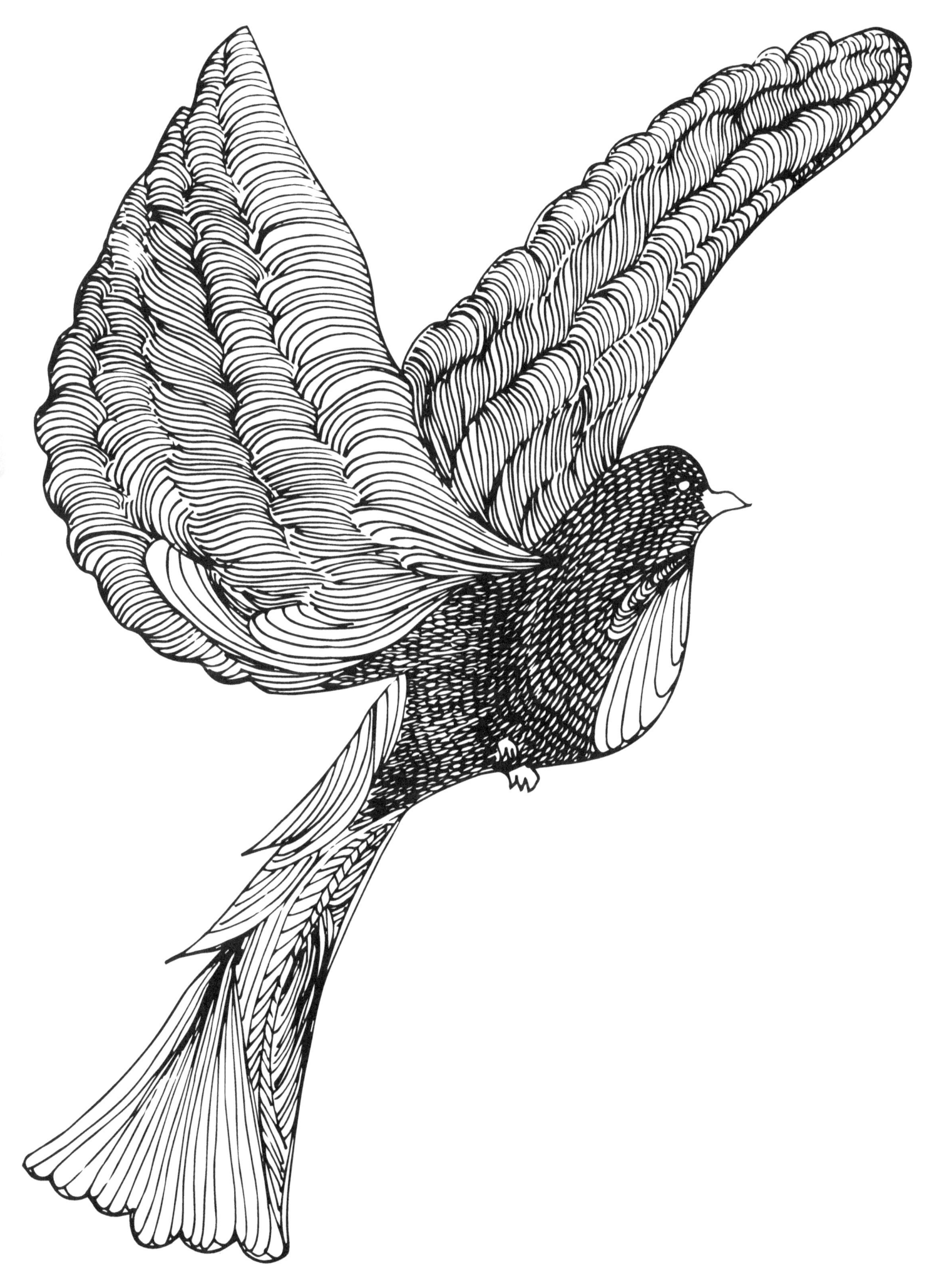

Contact Caron

Email: caron@hereugostudio.com

Web: hereugostudio.com

Facebook: facebook.com/hereugostudio

Pinterest: pinterest.com/hereugostudio

Instagram: instagram.com/hereugostudio

Share your creations with hereugostudio!
Take a photo of your work and upload it to Instagram. And don't forget to use the hashtag *#mytruecolors*.

www.ingramcontent.com/pod-product-compliance
Lightning Source LLC
Chambersburg PA
CBHW080827180526
45168CB00006B/2597